PEDRO
PIETRI

PEDRO

S E L E C T E D   P O E T R Y

PIETRI

Edited by Juan Flores and Pedro López Adorno

City Lights Books | San Francisco

Library of Congress Cataloging-in-Publication Data

Pietri, Pedro, 1944-2004.
  [Poems. Selections]
  Pedro Pietri : selected poetry / edited by Juan Flores and Pedro López
Adorno.
     pages cm
  ISBN 978-0-87286-656-0 (paperback)
  I. Flores, Juan, 1943-2014, editor. II. López-Adorno, Pedro, 1954- editor.
III. Title.

PS3566.I424A6 2015
811'.54—dc23

2015014713

City Lights Books are published at the City Lights Bookstore
261 Columbus Avenue, San Francisco, CA 94133
www.citylights.com

To Carmen Mercedes Pietri Díaz (1946-2015),
in memoriam.

CONTENTS

OUT OF ORDER

EL PARTY CONTINUES

LOVE POEMS TO MY SURREALIST GYPSY

LOOSE POEMS

PUERTO RICAN OBITUARY

PUERTO RICAN OBITUARY

They worked
They were always on time
They were never late
They never spoke back
when they were insulted
They worked
They never took days off
that were not on the calendar
They never went on strike
without permission
They worked
ten days a week
and were only paid for five
They worked
They worked
They worked
and they died
They died broke
They died owing
They died never knowing
what the front entrance
of the first national city bank looks like

Juan
Miguel
Milagros
Olga
Manuel
All died yesterday today
and will die again tomorrow
passing their bill collectors

on to the next of kin
All died
waiting for the garden of eden
to open up again
under a new management
All died
dreaming about america
waking them up in the middle of the night
screaming: Mira Mira
your name is on the winning lottery ticket
for one hundred thousand dollars
All died
hating the grocery stores
that sold them make-believe steak
and bullet-proof rice and beans
All died waiting dreaming and hating

Dead Puerto Ricans
Who never knew they were Puerto Ricans
Who never took a coffee break
from the ten commandments
to KILL KILL KILL
the landlords of their cracked skulls
and communicate with their latino souls

Juan
Miguel
Milagros
Olga
Manuel
From the nervous breakdown streets
where the mice live like millionaires
and the people do not live at all
are dead and were never alive

Juan
died waiting for his number to hit
Miguel
died waiting for the welfare check
to come and go and come again
Milagros
died waiting for her ten children
to grow up and work
so she could quit working
Olga
died waiting for a five dollar raise
Manuel
died waiting for his supervisor to drop dead
so he could get a promotion

Is a long ride
from Spanish Harlem
to long island cemetery
where they were buried
First the train
and then the bus
and the cold cuts for lunch
and the flowers
that will be stolen
when visiting hours are over
Is very expensive
Is very expensive
But they understand
Their parents understood
Is a long non-profit ride
from Spanish Harlem
to long island cemetery

Juan
Miguel
Milagros
Olga
Manuel
All died yesterday today
and will die again tomorrow
Dreaming
Dreaming about queens
Clean-cut lily-white neighborhood
Puerto Ricanless scene
Thirty-thousand-dollar home
The first spics on the block
Proud to belong to a community
of gringos who want them lynched
Proud to be a long distance away
from the sacred phrase: Que Pasa

These dreams
These empty dreams
from the make-believe bedrooms
their parents left them
are the after-effects
of television programs
about the ideal
white american family
with black maids
and latino janitors
who are well train—
to make everyone
and their bill collectors
laugh at them
and the people they represent

Juan
died dreaming about a new car
Miguel
died dreaming about new anti-poverty programs
Milagros
died dreaming about a trip to Puerto Rico
Olga
died dreaming about real jewelry
Manuel
died dreaming about the irish sweepstakes

They all died
like a hero sandwich dies
in the garment district
at twelve o'clock in the afternoon
social security number to ashes
union dues to dust

They knew
they were born to weep
and keep the morticians employed
as long as they pledge allegiance
to the flag that wants them destroyed
They saw their names listed
in the telephone directory of destruction
They were train to turn
the other cheek by newspapers
that mispelled mispronounced
and misunderstood their names
and celebrated when death came
and stole their final laundry ticket

They were born dead
and they died dead
Is time
to visit sister lopez again
the number one healer
and fortune card dealer
in Spanish Harlem
She can communicate
with your late relatives
for a reasonable fee
Good news is guaranteed
Rise Table Rise Table
death is not dumb and disable—
Those who love you want to know
the correct number to play
Let them know this right away
Rise Table Rise Table
death is not dumb and disable
Now that your problems are over
and the world is off your shoulders
help those who you left behind
find financial peace of mind
Rise Table Rise Table
death is not dumb and disable
If the right number we hit
all our problems will split
and we will visit your grave
on every legal holiday
Those who love you want to know
the correct number to play
Let them know this right away
We know your spirit is able
Death is not dumb and disable
RISE TABLE RISE TABLE

Juan
Miguel
Milagros
Olga
Manuel
All died yesterday today
and will die again tomorrow
Hating fighting and stealing
broken windows from each other
Practicing a religion without a roof
The old testament
The new testament
according to the gospel
of the internal revenue
the judge and jury and executioner
protector and eternal bill collector

Secondhand shit for sale
Learn how to say Como Esta Usted
and you will make a fortune
They are dead
They are dead
and will not return from the dead
until they stop neglecting
the art of their dialogue—
for broken english lessons
to impress the mister goldsteins—
who keep them employed
as lavaplatos porters messenger boys
factory workers maids stock clerks
shipping clerks assistant mailroom
assistant, assistant assistant
to the assistant's assistant
assistant lavaplatos and automatic

artificial smiling doormen
for the lowest wages of the ages
and rages when you demand a raise
because *is* against the company policy
to promote SPICS SPICS SPICS

Juan
died hating Miguel because Miguel's
used car was in better running condition
than his used car
Miguel
died hating Milagros because Milagros
had a color television set
and he could not afford one yet
Milagros
died hating Olga because Olga
made five dollars more on the same job
Olga
died hating Manuel because Manuel
had hit the numbers more times
than she had hit the numbers
Manuel
died hating all of them
Juan
Miguel
Milagros
and Olga
because they all spoke broken english
more fluently than he did

And now they are together
in the main lobby of the void
Addicted to silence
Off limits to the wind

Confined to worm supremacy
in long island cemetery
This is the groovy hereafter
the protestant collection box
was talking so loud and proud about

Here lies Juan
Here lies Miguel
Here lies Milagros
Here lies Olga
Here lies Manuel
who died yesterday today
and will die again tomorrow
Always broke
Always owing
Never knowing
that they are beautiful people
Never knowing
the geography of their complexion

PUERTO RICO IS A BEAUTIFUL PLACE
PUERTORRIQUENOS ARE A BEAUTIFUL RACE
If only they
had turned off the television
and tune into their own imaginations
If only they
had used the white supremacy bibles
for toilet paper purpose
and make their latino souls
the only religion of their race
If only they
had return to the definition of the sun
after the first mental snowstorm

on the summer of their senses
If only they
had kept their eyes open
at the funeral of their fellow employees
who came to this country to make a fortune
and were buried without underwears

Juan
Miguel
Milagros
Olga
Manuel
will right now be doing their own thing
where beautiful people sing
and dance and work together
where the wind is a stranger
to miserable weather conditions
where you do not need a dictionary
to communicate with your people
Aqui
Se Habla Espanol
all the time
Aqui you salute your flag first
Aqui there are no dial soap commercials
Aqui everybody smells good
Aqui tv dinners do not have a future
Aqui the men and women admire desire
and never get tired of each other
Aqui Que Pasa Power is what's happening
Aqui to be called negrito
means to be called LOVE

THE BROKEN ENGLISH DREAM

It was the night
before the welfare check
and everybody sat around the table
hungry heartbroken cold confused
and unable to heal the wounds
on the dead calendar of our eyes
Old newspapers and empty beer cans
and jesus is the master of this house
Picture frames made in japan by the u.s.
was hanging out in the kitchen
which was also the livingroom
the bedroom and the linen closet
Wall to wall bad news was playing
over the radio that last week was stolen
by dying dope addicts looking for a fix
to forget that they were ever born
The slumlord came with hand grenades
in his bad breath to collect the rent
we were unable to pay six month ago
and inform us and all the empty
shopping bags we own that unless
we pay we will be evicted immediately
And the streets where the night lives
and the temperature is below zero
three hundred sixty-five days a year
will become our next home address
All the lightbulbs of our apartment
were left and forgotten at the pawnshop
across the street from the heart attack

the broken back buildings were having
Infants not born yet played hide n seek
in the cemetery of their imagination
Blind in the mind tenants were praying
for numbers to hit so they can move out
and wake up with new birth certificates
The grocery stores were outnumbered by
funeral parlors with neon signs that said
Customers wanted No experience necessary
A liquor store here and a liquor store
everywhere you looked filled the polluted
air with on the job training prostitutes
pimps and winos and thieves and abortions
White business store owners from clean-cut
plush push-button neat neighborhoods
who learn how to speak spanish in six weeks
wrote love letters to their cash registers
Vote for me! said the undertaker: I am
the man with the solution to your problems

To the united states we came
To learn how to mispell our name
To lose the definition of pride
To have misfortune on our side
To live where rats and roaches roam
in a house that is definitely not a home
To be trained to turn on television sets
To dream about jobs you will never get
To fill out welfare applications
To graduate from school without an education
To be drafted distorted and destroyed
To work full time and still be unemployed

To wait for income tax returns
and stay drunk and lose concern
for the heart and soul of our race
and the climate that produce our face

To pledge allegiance
to the flag
of the united states
of installment plans
One nation
under discrimination
for which it stands
and which it falls
with poverty injustice
and televised
firing squads
for everyone who has
the sun on the side
of their complexion

Lapiz: Pencil
Pluma: Pen
Cocina: Kitchen
Gallina: Hen

Everyone who learns this
will receive a high school equivalency diploma
a lifetime supply of employment agencies
a different bill collector for every day of the week
the right to vote for the executioner of your choice
and two hamburgers for thirty-five cents in times square

We got off
the two-engine airplane
at idlewild airport
(re-named kennedy airport
twenty years later)
with all our furniture
and personal belongings
in our back pockets

We follow the sign
that says welcome to america
but keep your hands
off the property
violators will be electrocuted
follow the garbage truck
to the welfare department
if you cannot speak english

So this is america
land of the free
for everybody
but our family
So this is america
where you wake up
in the morning
to brush your teeth
with the home relief
the leading toothpaste
operation bootstrap
promise you you will get
every time you buy
a box of cornflakes

on the lay-away plan
So this is america
land of the free
to watch the
adventures of superman
on tv if you know
somebody who owns a set
that works properly
So this is america
exploited by columbus
in fourteen ninety-two
with captain video
and lady bird johnson
the first miss subways
in the new testament
So this is america
where they keep you
busy singing
en mi casa toman bustelo
en mi casa toman bustelo

BEWARE OF SIGNS

Beware of signs that say
"Aqui Se Habla Espanol"
Dollar Down Dollar A Week
until your dying days

BUEYNOS DIASS
COMO ESTA YOUSTED?
AQUI SAY FIA
MUEBLAYRIA
Y TELEVECION SETS
ROPAS BARRATOS
TRAJES Y ZAPATOS
PARA SUSHIJOS
AND YOUR MARIDOS
NUMAYROSAS COSA
PARA LA ESPOSA
KAY TIENAY TODO
KAY BUEYNO CREDITO
PUEDAY COMPRAR
MACHINAS DAY LAVAR
VACUM CLEANEROS
YOUSTED NAME IT
AND IF NOSOTROS
NO LO TENAYMOS
WE LO INVENTAYMOS
IMMEDIATAMENTAY
JESS WE WILL
NADUAQUIESIMPOSI
BLAYBLABLUDAGHAZ

OOLADUYAJAYEAHAZ
SI NO SAY NECESITA
NINGUNO DINEROS
SOLAMENTAY YOU SIGN
AQUI ON THIS LINE
Y TODO WILL BE FINE
MUCHAS GRACIAS SENOR
MUCHAS GRACIAS SENORA
AND DON'T FORGET
TO VUELVAY AGAIN
TELL ALL YOUR NEXT
DOOR VEYCINOS THAT
WITH EVERY TEN DOLLAR
PURCHASE THEY MAKE
LEY DEMOS UNO DISCO
DEY LA CANCION
DEY SU FAVORITO
TELEVICION PROGRAMA
simpleymentay maria
simpleymentay maria
maria maria ETCETRA
HASTA LA VISTO AMIGO

Beware of signs that say
"Aqui Se Habla Espanol"
Do not go near those places
of smiling faces that do not smile
and bill collectors who are well train
to forget how to habla espanol
when you fall back on those weekly payments

Beware! Be wise! Do not patronize
Garbage is all they are selling you
Here today gone tomorrow merchandise

You wonder where your bedroom set went
after you make the third payment

Those bastards should be sued
for false advertisement
What they talk no es espanol
What they talk is alotta BULLSHIT

SUICIDE NOTE FROM A COCKROACH IN A LOW INCOME HOUSING PROJECT

I hate the world
I am depress
I am deprive
I am deprave
I am ready to propose to the grave
Life is too complicated to proceed
Fate is the only medicine I need to feel good

Seriously speaking
I am seriously seeking
the exit to leave this eerie existence
My resistance is low and will not grow

Rent control my ghost will haunt you

I hate the world
I am dejected
I am rejected
I am neglected and disrespected
ever since these damn liberals got elected
and corrected nothing really important
I am starving
I am no good at robbing
I have no ambitions
These damn housing projects
are responsible for my nervous condition

I hate you credit cards
Because of you there is a pain in my brain
Because of you all the minority groups

own a television set and will not let me sleep
at night watching the late show at full blast

I hate the world
I hate the world
I hate the world
I am disgusted
I am totally busted
The welfare department
will not handle my case
I am homesick for the past
when radio use to be a luxury
for the minority groups
and there were no such things as the late late show
Oh how I hate those damn
anti-poverty programs

All those electric appliances
are executing my people
If only the tenants knew
it was bad and destructive for them too
the world would be a better place
for everyone regardless of race
END THE WAR ON POVERTY NOW
before our race is erased from the face
of every place
We do not want to be
destroy diminish and finish forever america
I am hungry
My folks are hungry
My friends are hungry
Every member of our generation
is a victim of starvation
We are down and out without a future

to look forward to WE ARE THROUGH
I attend over ten funerals every day
I don't have time to send my black
melancholy suit to the cleaners anymore
That is how bad the situation is
and all because all of a sudden
everybody wants to be somebody
This is ridiculous this is absurd
why should our race be erased to make
america a beautiful place for everyone but us

We are the real american
We was here before columbus
We was here before general electric
We was here before the ed sullivan show
We are older than adam and eve
Noah also took cockroaches into his ark
Why should we be denied coexistence???

Back in the old days
long before these housing projects
wrecked our civilization
cockroaches were strangers to starvation
and lived better than the pepsi generation
There was always enough to eat for everybody
Every day was a holiday in those days

Those were the days my friend
we thought will never end
We use to eat forever every day
Our problems were few
No bill collectors no internal revenue
Those were the days oh yes those were the days

The life expectancy
of a cockroach in those days
was ten times longer than it is today
Ten seconds to ten minutes is the new limit
These damn anti-poverty programs are to blame
Since they came the people are not the same
Today everyone can afford the price of DDT
DEATH IS JUST A SPRAY AWAY
the television commercial says
Everyone old enough to talk is being train
to use deadly weapons to wipe us out

THIS IS GENOCIDE
And what bothers me the most
is that nobody is protesting
No demonstrations no moratorium for our dead
Everybody is busy protesting this
Everybody is busy protesting that
Everybody is raising hell about the air strikes
But nobody is saying a damn thing about the DDT strikes
Like nobody is wearing STOP THE DDT STRIKE buttons

I use to come
from a very large family
and now I am down
to my last second cousin in-law
I have been married seven times
I have never been divorced
All my wives and husbands
are now resting in peace
None of them died from natural cause
They have all been fatal casualties
of the games the great society plays

This so-called civilization nation
has made a lonely man out of me

My insurance company
has informed me that they will not
insure another wife or husband I take
They think I am trying to make
a living out of this THEY ARE DEAD WRONG
I come from a good non-catholic
non-protestant non-jewish home

I have never read the holy bible
I will never read the holy bible
Cockroaches in their right minds
will never go near the holy bible
Bible reading is a dangerous mission
Is like committing suicide to get to heaven

I once had this uncle
who was very religious
He read the good book all the time
One day he fell asleep reading
the twenty-third psalm and woke up
in the hereafter the following morning
The owner of the bible close the book on him

I once knew this clairol lady
who threw salt and pepper on my people
and fed them to her pet hamster

I once knew this marlboro man
who decorated his ashtrays with my people
after putting his cigarettes out on them

I once knew this boy
who married the clairol lady
and gave birth to the marlboro man
His mission in life magazine
was to sell us gasoline in listerine bottles

If those are the kind of people
that go to heaven you can send me to hell lord

I want to be
a million miles away from humanity
with their vanity and profanity
and insanity preachers preaching survival
for them and the hell with everybody else
who cannot read the new york times
drink good booze have the wall street blues
hate discriminate castigate castrate
liquidate assassinate and instigate air pollution
oppose revolutions that will put a conclusion
to confusion and welcome positive solutions
end false illusions of the beginning of time
I want to be a million miles away
from nickles and dimes and quarters
and dollars white collars bright collars
blue collars go screw yourself collars
millionaires carfares welfares nightmares
and all that neurotic psychotic idiotic
chaotic air of despair found everywhere
underwears of deception win the elections
If I have to sin to make this wish come true
I will start by saying: our father
which art in heaven FUCK YOU

My first wife
lived a very short life
Tragedy came
separated our name
The first year
we started our atmosphere
she was ambush
by this retarded boy
who destroyed her pride
and swallow her body
after she died

My second wife
lived a shorter life
When tragedy came
and separated our name
she was still a virgin
We were married in the afternoon
and somebody stepped on her
on our way to the honeymoon

My third wife
was taking a short-cut home
thru the kitchen sink
A homicidal maniac saw her
while taking a drink
and turned on the hot water

My fourth wife
was a militant
She carried a knife
and was prepare
to cut anyone up

who threaten her life
She said to me
on our wedding night
I know I know
someday I have to go
but not without a fight
Before they kill me
I will have three
or more of them on the floor
ready for the morgue
The following day
she passed away
on a crowded elevator
I warn her to beware
of those modern inventions
but she paid no attention
If she had used the stairs
she would still be
alive and well with me

My first husband
lost his sacred life
in a DDT strike
coming home from the A&P
for insects only
I was in tears
for one whole year
after he disappear
from the atmosphere
because the day before
his destiny came near
his insurance policy lapse
I mailed a payment
a week before he died

but somebody stepped on the mailman
and the payment never arrived

My second husband
was suffocated
by this complicated
mentally constipated
fire engine impersonator
who got his kicks
kidnapping cockroaches
molesting them sexually
and throwing them
into empty coca-cola bottles
and putting the cap back on
and keeping them without air
until their life was gone

Oh why did not the earth
have an abortion
when all these fatalistic
sons and daughters
of tv dinners were born

The republican party
the democratic party
con edison general electric
gillete razor blades playtex
general motors and all
those other deadly odors
blessed by the daily news
should take an overdose
of that birth control pill
their test tube minds
invented in their spare time

and stop that fatal disease
called civilization
from destroying the nation

My third husband
lived a miserable life
He had lung cancer
ten wooden legs
one glass eye
fifty-fifty vision
in his good eye
a weak heart
a broken back
respiratory ailment
undernourished
mentally discourage
unemployed eardrums
condem features
and bad breath galore
from a bottle of
weight reducing pills
he shoplifted
at the drugstore
I gave him a divorce
not because his health
was hazardous
to my health
I gave him a divorce
because he wanted
me to sell my body
to science
and give him the money
for plastic surgery
One week before

celebrating his last
unhappy birthday
at the funeral parlor
he hit the numbers
for one thousand dollars
went to the hospital
and paid cash for
a heart transplant
an eyes transplant
a face transplant
a legs transplant
o lung transplant
o rear end transplant
a breath transplant
And he was all set
to live and let live
for one hundred years
but on his way home
from the hospital
somebody stepped on him
and that was the end
of his breathing career

So you see
you cannot really blame me
for wanting to seduce my destiny
I have nothing else to live for
in this corrupted world anymore
The employment situation is bad
The starvation situation is worse
It hurts to continue living like this
Cockroaches are starving to death
ever since incinerators come
into the life of the minority groups

In the old buildings the people
were very close to everything they had
Food was never thrown away
But today everything is going
into those incinerators
The last family that lived here
took the incinerator
to get to the first floor
They do not live here anymore
Damn these low income housing projects
Years ago suicide was never spoken
but today suicide is a luxury
for a heartbroken cockroach
trying to make a decent living
in a low income housing project

Goodbye cruel world
I am thru being screw
by your crossword puzzles
When the bomb comes down
I will not be around
Forward my mail to your conscience when you get one

TATA

Mi abuela
has been
in this dept store
called america
for the past twenty-five years
She is eighty-five years old
and does not speak
a word of english

That is intelligence

TRAFFIC
VIOLATIONS

JANUARY HANGOVER

To be with you is my desire
To stay away from you is my ambition
The magic of your great moments
Awakens the superior inspiration
Responsible for perfect compliments
We have many things to talk about
And we have nothing to talk about
The religion of the sleepless candle
Detaining the discovery of daylight
When the definition of madness is love
Was lit by your knowledge of darkness
Your comfort corrects all the mistakes
I was born to make in this world
You are a very simple person
With a very complicated personality
Uninvited visitors with visions
Of watering your plants everyday
Commit suicide to write poems about you
It is impossible to love you madly
Without actually loving you madly
For the best results of your secrets
Of summer I will sacrifice my sanity
And become brilliantly absentminded
To remember how much I adore you

MARCH HANGOVER

I am mad
I am very mad
This behavior is not unusual
This is the normal way to act
When you are too busy doing nothing
To take down notes of all
The crazy statements in your head
I must run around the block slowly
To avoid hurting anybody's feelings
I am not acting strange
I still remember many things
That everybody else has forgotten
To leave your apartment
You must open the door first
This is the reason why
I am the only madman in the street
When everybody else is fast asleep
Dreaming they had the courage
To stop laughing at my jokes
For no reason at all I punch walls
When I am in a good mood
If a man or a woman insults me
I will do my best to destroy them
If I am praised I will do likewise
This is how late I stay awake
I must run around the block quickly
Now that you know this much about me
And don't forget to mention
That on the 7th day I rested
Don't get the wrong impression

I am definitely not into jogging
When I move I don't go anywhere
Haven't left this block in years
I pick up speed and stand still
And relax without changing the subject
That will bring forth another day
To forget what was left undone
After the smoke & the rum
Kept me laughing at everyone

MAY HANGOVER

There were many conversations
We were driven crazy to share
Those many last nights we are
In the slow process of forgetting

When it was important to say
Something that makes no sense
To stay calm and indifferent
In those times of total strangers

In a season when it was safe
to stare away from glass mirrors
And let the wind comb your hair
In preparation for total silence

To be able to know each other
Without having to exchange names
And the songs sing themselves
And the poems imagine their fame

OCTOBER HANGOVER

I pledge allegiance to poetry
Co pilot of eternal daydreamers
Of fame that brings no fortune
Into the coherent religion
Of intoxicated individuals
Dressed in long blank feelings
At the altar of lost memories
Where wild insomniacs celebrate
The high mass for the drunken
Defectors of the break of dawn
Falling out of wounded mirrors
After levitating indefinitely
From heavenly orgasms in hell
Where they slept with the widow
Of the creator of the universe
After their liberty was limited
By the disciples of undertakers
Who laughed at the myth makers
When they lost their manuscripts
Staggering in the heavy traffic
Of false illusions where the wind
Is determine to never blow
Lord have mercy on their souls
Who have ceased sleeping forever
To walk the streets at night
In the darker idea of paradise
Where original outlaws confess
They are the supreme lunatics

In the society of shut eyes
Whose mission is to immortalize
Those who are thru pretending
There's an ending to the madness

DECEMBER HANGOVER

And now that at last slow and fast
You have accomplished your mission
Of drinking everyone under the table
You can become the missing person
You always imagined yourself to be

You have nothing to worry about
You can respond to whatever name
You are called by affable back stabbers
Who not too long ago drank together
With you when you were never you

You can lower your head up high now
You can tremble with your empty hands
You can succeed in losing your memory
To keep warm before and after the storm
Where time and space become orphans

Your unwritten poems will outlive you
And never forgive you for leaving them
Incomplete to detain your induction
Into the circle of the most forgotten
Heads of states of their lost minds

Now that nobody admires you anymore
You can stop drinking so much and wait
For the traffic light to change before
Staying right where you are to decide
What to do when you finally sober up

TRAFFIC VIOLATIONS

you go into chicken delight
and order dinosaurs
because you are hungry
and want something different
now that you no longer
eat meat or fish or vegetables

you are told politely
is against company policies
to be that different
so you remove a button off
your absentminded overcoat
the scenery changes
you are waiting in line
to take a mean leak
at one of those public toilets
in the times square area
the line is 3 weeks long
many waited with their lunch
inside brown paper bags
singing the battle hymn
of the republic to keep warm

you remove another button off
your absentminded overcoat
all you can see now are
high heels and low quarter shoes
coming at your eyeballs
disappearing when they come
close enough to make contact

you try to get up off the floor
but you forgot how to move
umbrellas open up inside your head
you start screaming backwards
your legs behave like flat tires
your mind melts in slow motion

you remove another button off
your absentminded overcoat
is late in the evening
according to everybody
who keeps track of time
you are about to jump off the roof
emergency sirens are heard

A crowd of skilled & unskilled
Laborers on their mental lunch break
congregate on the street below
the roof you are about to jump from
they are laughing hysterically
nobody tries to talk you out of it
everybody wants you to jump
so they can get some sleep tonight—
should you change your mind about jumping
All the spectators will get uptight

red white and blue representatives
from the suicide prevention bureau
order you to jump immediately
you refuse to obey their orders
they sendout a helicopter to push you
off the roof into the morning headlines
the laughter from the crowd
on the street breaks the sound barrier

you try removing another button off
your absentminded overcoat
but that button is reported missing
the helicopter pushes you off the roof
everybody is feeling much better
you are losing your memory real fast
the clouds put on black arm bands
it starts raining needles and thread

a few seconds before having breakfast
at a cafeteria in the hereafter
you remove your absentminded overcoat

you are on the front and back seat
of a bi-lingo spaceship
smoking grass with your friends
from the past present and future
nothing unusual is happening
you are all speeding
without moving an inch
making sure nobody does the driving

INTERMISSION FROM MONDAY

have to leave the city
because sidewalks are sidewalks
parking meters are parking meters
and heavy traffic is very heavy
I know I will miss myself very much
every single second I am not around
but if I don't get out of town
blank walls might become blank walls
and that I cannot tolerate at all

have to leave the city
before my breakfast gets suspicious
and calls an ambulance to take me away
applauding a battle that was lost
because it made society safe for anxiety
O my lunch will be extremely lonely
and get cold and have to be discarded
when I am not around to stare at it
in the presence of gigantic noise makers

have to leave the city
when what you see is what you see
and what you don't see you don't see
and the imagination is classified
as excess luggage at the airport
where picture frames are picture frames
and the lines get longer and longer
for first class tickets on a bookshelf
where a poet has become a poet
to everyone except himself

INTERMISSION FROM WEDNESDAY

I expect to be praised
Everytime a ship sinks in the sea
And there are no survivors
To talk about the good old days
To the unborn they left behind
In the ruins of psychological cradles
Rocking from one planet to the next
Where the highest compliment I expect
When the high priest of psychiatric ward
Wears a black hood over his straightjacket
To make the patients laugh & cry & when
The joke finally ends to snap again
In the presence of relatives & friends
You swear you never saw before in your
Brilliant career of being a scatter brain
Who felt no pain when you jumped all the way
Up to the top of the Empire State Building
To ask one of the employees for a match
To start a fire never to be controlled
& I will hold a press conference in City Hall
For the reward I am to receive for not
Reporting the event to the fire department
Until everybody is hard of hearing
& have impaired visions of immortality
& praise me for taking full responsibility
For a tragedy that could have been prevented
If someone had invented this country
Instead of discovering & destroying it
To call it their land & your land too
If the medication works on you

INTERMISSION FROM THURSDAY

I am being followed by a table
And there is nowhere to hide

This happened all of a sudden
I was minding my own business
Listening to a record that skips
Back and forth for five weeks

When suddenly I noticed
The table giving me a mean look
Without me having said or done
Anything to offend the table

At first I paid no attention
But then I noticed the table
Coming close & closer towards me
Until our legs were touching
I decided to go out for a walk
And when I got downstairs
The table was there waiting for me
So I immediately went back UP

And to the astonishing surprise
Of these hands and these eyes
I found the table waiting for me
At the entrance of my front door
The record continues to skip
The table will not let me enter
And all I can do about it
Is to snap my fingers and hope
I am making this whole thing up

So I can get back inside and play
A record that doesn't skip

1 A.M. NEVER AGAIN

we returned from those mountains
we have never been to before
the daydreaming finally ended
we made contact with the floor
the earth became the earth
the sky was always the sky
you were never a real person
though there were tears in your eyes
and a climate in your inner self
it was me and nobody else
whose hands I held very tight
to protect me from total strangers
who kept shouting let there be light
so I will not be able to see
that empty room of my dreams
and go through life pretending
love will keep me from being lonely
oh how foolish of me to think
I could function without a drink
and see flames inside a mirror
without lit candles to expand
the mad mind of this madder man
who knows how to dance very wrong
in other planets all night long
looking for comfort from a ghost
who once loved him the most
until the sun came out in the day
and the night had to go away
making poems impossible to occur
in words soft enough to disappear

into the invisible shadow of
A breeze that leads to solitude
in the arms of someone very dear
who once made everything very clear
and kept the clouds undressed
so that we didn't have to impress
each other before and after
the decision to become true lovers
for better or worse into bliss
to prove that magic does exist

1ST UNTITLED POEM

Looking for something I had lost
I came across a flawless blank page
That impressed me to the point
Of where I found myself losing sleep
Over this original piece of paper
That explains nothing whatsoever

I instructed myself to write a poem
On this magnificent blank page
That has occupied every single second
I find myself in deep concentration
When the world outside my head stops
To answer questions I ask in my sleep

I know that writing this poem
Will be extremely complicated for me
Regardless of my traffic violations
Due to the facts of the temptation
To protect this perfect statement
Whose authenticity I'll testify for

I have an important decision to make
That will change my life around
I know it will be very unwise of me
To lose sleep over writing this poem
When the correct thing for me to do
Is to lose sleep keeping the page blank

5TH UNTITLED POEM

all numbers are odd numbers
in the history of unfamiliar horizon
where quaint travelers sleepwalk
on the surface of the harbor
carrying odd suitcases in one hand
and huge flashlights in the other

they have been invited to attend
the opening night of abandoned vehicles
and semi lit lamp posts suspended
in mid-air above the deeper dark waters
of the strange river they are crossing
dressed for very hot and cold weather

naked children ride their shoulders
blindfolding them with the palms
of their hands in a surgical cast
from wounds inflicted in the womb

these infants are the circus freaks
the frustrated elated travelers seek
who have traveled far and sacrificed much
and will do a complete about face when
they finally reach their destination

to avoid practicing what they preach
from the last floor of bar stools
where slow records are heard louder
and prophets actually fall off trees
and land in bottomless cradles crazy

vomiting pieces of birth certificates
the size and color of snowflakes
singing the lord's prayer to the tune
of hare krishna hare krishna a-men

until they convince themselves
they have no more automatic feelings
and look down from the ceiling
and see business going on as usual
and wonder how did everybody get there
from the pages of a lost manuscript

8TH UNTITLED POEM

nothing old will ever
be accomplished as long as there
are lines on the written page
to read inbetween from

save all your compliments
and praises and angry insults
for everyone including yourself
should you be reading this poem

on this page that once
had the privilege to be blank
until the night I got drunk
and was unable to write anything

I know most people think
this exercise is possible sometimes
but I know it is quite impossible
all the time of being possible

it was never done before
and should I accomplish it now
I will definitely get bored

so then in the meantime
there is a bottle of cold wine
and some cheese in the refrigerator
feel free to help yourself to some

drink without removing the cork
if you want to get invited back

10TH UNTITLED POEM

I admit I have always wanted
to be as difficult as possible
& have no respect for authority
So I won't be mistreated by anybody
And grow up to stay very young
And visit my great grandchildren
In a nursing home for the aged
Whose minds can no-longer expand
Regardless of what drugs they take

I am not content with myself
Unless I disagree with everybody
It doesn't matter if they are right
I will always swear they are wrong
So they may drop dead before me
Trying to get a concrete point across
That I of course will be erasing
In front of them or when their backs
Are turned for someone to stab them

I cross against the traffic
Not to get runover by a vehicle
But to insult the driver & passenger
For not walking & talking to themselves
On week days & weekends & days off
In public & be called ridiculous
By myself & other normal people
Who take seven hour lunch breaks
& just put in one hour on the job

I will work very hard on a poem
& leave construction work to others
Whose mothers & fathers disowned them
For not growing up to rule the world
I oppose leaders & their followers
Support fire eaters & sword swallowers
Don't expect me to explain anything
All I can truly say about myself
Is that after monday comes tuesday

13TH UNTITLED POEM

the sky is every other color but blue
as I sit and wonder what to type next
on this official blank sheet of paper
reserved for poetry and nothing else

I have no plans for today or tomorrow
the walls have already been stared at
Everything is understood misunderstood
I can only plan for the past these days

should my pencil drop on the floor
I might decide to pick it up or not
to take credit for important decisions
and be warmly embraced by my shadow

these are the better moments I've had
all year long of not knowing what day
of the week it is or the correct time
of a poem that hasn't been written yet

to make a short story shorter I will
not say another word and rise from
the chair I am sitting on to stretch
my arms outwards and then sitbackdown

to wonder if anybody that I know now
and won't know much later on in life
missed me very much in those fewer
seconds I was away from my typewriter

CONVERSATION IN A DARKER ROOM

With or without your permission
I promise to tremble at your presence
And deliberately say the wrong things
Trying my very best to impress you
To experience superb panic in paradise
Praising the details that define you
Who will be loved madly all the time
During the gentle and violent ceremony
Of losing our minds to find each other
And take credit for knowing everything
There is to know about feeling terrific
When the world ends for everyone but us
Tossing and turning forever together
In explicit evidence of enthusiasm
For the rules & violations of pleasure
All the days of our lives in a second
That will outlive the entire universe

APRIL 15TH UNTIL FURTHER NOTICE

the 15th of april imagine that
for it will always be this day of the week
all the nights you speak a foreign language
in all the conversations you were born to have
with shoplifters of your equilibrium
in all the dreams you wake up screaming from
after her night gown spins you around
and she steals your breath into her breast
from then on everytime you shut your eyes
it will be new year's eve all over again
and your father is very drunk
and your mother is very upset
and the children pretend they are morticians
with ambitions to be rich and famous
though it was the 31st of december on all
the calendars in graveyard walls
we are talking about the 15th of april
a nice day to go to the airport
and beg the ticket agent for last rites
because tho some waitress loves your very much
she will only go to bed with a hero sandwich
so drink your black coffee in peace
if poetry was born to write about you
the employment agencies will know about it
and you will have more than an hour for lunch

the 15th of april imagine that
nothing out of the ordinary was happening
in the world of walking canes & pace makers
in the future of mandatory parkbenches

for gala gatherings of senior citizens destined
to stare out-into-space indefinitely—
I complained about the price of the drinks
and though the barmaid loves me very much
she will not let me touch her contact lenses
so I counted the faded poetic details
of the fallen leaves of the lost memory
of a Season that only comes to the mind
when you find yourself with nothing to say
to a special person on a special occasion
of holding hands and dropping dead my dear
because nothing will ever again be clear
the earth is not where the earth is at

the 15th of april imagine that
my appetite for the absence of light
was obvious in your wounded emotions
like always I was wrong and you were right
but this time your hair was short
it was for that reason & that reason only
that I had the courage to hurt your feelings
while kneeling before you in thoughts
of a perfect ocean for us to drown in
dressed as clouds from another experience
in the neighborhood of the incredible
where I see you and I don't see you

imagine that the 15th of april
is the first day of the new decade
& you will not be thirty years old soon
because you are destine to get younger
while I order another drink & another one
& another one after that one until or else

& otherwise I can be honest about the lies
I was born to tell you all the days
of all the ashtrays of your household
where I know you and I don't know you

of april the 15th imagine that
you have just entered a cafeteria
with many endless questions to ask me
because I have all the answers
because I love you with all my heart
because I hate you with all my metaphor
because we are here and not here
because the menu has instructed us to stare
and not eat what we came here to order
nor are we allowed to drink the water
and the waitress & waiters are blindfolded
because they are unskilled laborers
and by not actually seeing what they do
for a living they can fantasize
they are driven to work in limousines
by midgets that moonlight as chauffeurs
and because their legs are too short
for the accelerator & the mergency breaks
they take you nowhere all day long
and what they are doing isn't wrong

imagine of april the 15th that—
imagine a few other things also
but always keep in mind what day
of the week it will always be
minus you minus me minus everybody
who won't live forever for refusing

to acknowledge they were born
to hold each other very tight
under an umbrella on the beach
after the war was imagined over
& the drunks dance with lifeless
casualties of the easter parade
who thought they had it made in life
because their uniforms looked nice
but don't let anything that I say
interrupt your plans for this day
you have nothing to worry about baby
your fear of becoming a shopping bag lady
is all in your no vacancy sign mind
the whole world knows you are fine
you motivate children to contemplate
necrophilia on afternoon school picnics
should you decide not to live forever
you will never age as long as your hair
stays long enough to induce amnesia
in the poet that admires you the most
and has all sacred intentions of sooner
or later seducing the ghost inside you
imagine that of april the 15th

happy new year to your eyes
happy new year to your lips
happy new year to your tits
happy new year to your legs
happy new year to your hips

lets get lost in our fingertips
together we will have a climactic trip
going nowhere and not returning

until we admit we are learning nothing
on this day that is this day again
& again until another year ends
in the history of mistreating everybody
on the 15th of April imagine that?

right now I am lying to you
later on the lies will get bigger
& bigger until I believe them myself
who wants you with nobody else
but me when I am present & absent
because though the meter maid loves me
more than she loves her terrible job
she will still make life hard for me
if I double park my car in her bedroom
so you see there is nothing to see
it's us who are they and them and we
on our knees at war praying for
an empty bar stool in the overcrowded
red light district of neon eternity
because maternity wards don't serve
alcohol to indestructable minors
to look their very worst since birth
& feel their very best since death
on April of the 15th imagine that
you should have stayed home
you should have never answered the phone
when I called up to apologize to you
for having done nothing out of the ordinary
why the hell were you at home?
why didn't you hang up the telephone
when I insisted today was a few years ago
when you let a total stranger starve

to death because he wanted to caress you
and rescue you from a terminal illness
called punctuation in some foreign nations
where the imagination is off limits
and anybody born on the 15th of april
will not be invited to their birthday party
and anybody who dies on the 15th of april
will not be invited to their own funeral?

the 15th of april imagine that
the white dress you wore last night
was very proud of the way it looked on you
those who contradict themselves
when it gets dark enough to see clearly
witness your presence inside the shut eyes
of the wrong bride they embraced
it was your face and the warm moments
of your breath they saw and heard
in the unclear words they whispered
to the ears they wish were yours to hear
the enthusiasm your punishment inspires

I am talking to myself again
and you have no choice but to listen
I agree with everything you say
everybody is gifted in whatsoever way
but only a poet is granted poetry
the rest are condemn to reoccurring prose
to feel significant about themselves
on legal traditional holidays only
the rest of the week they cannot speak
unless they are not spoken to
so you *see* what you *hear* isn't weird

though I love you much less this year
I'm still speechless when you are near
because even though the voice that says
there appears to be a receiver
off the phone thinks I am incredible
your bedroom is the only dark alley
I can pray for peace & panic & immortality
all the great days & memorable nights
of the 15th of april imagine that

MANUAL TYPEWRITER REVISITED

How strange the broom
Sweeping the floor
Minus the assistance
Of unskilled laborer
Or bank president
Bitter at the world
Everytime it gets dark
And crazy poets start
Making no sense at all
To complete a poem
For all those people
In a foreign forest
Where nothing is green
And everyone is broke
To avoid being persecuted
For making the mistake
Of spelling correctly

IN PRAISE OF A TOTAL STRANGER

Because your name I will never know
Because you might not even exist
I have taken time out from doing nothing
To talk highly of your achievements
And the fact that you are convinced nobody
Remembers what size shoes they take anymore
Because you don't have to know anything
About your defunct next door neighbor
To sweat and tremble on identical nights
In the autumn of short sleeve shirts
And unemotional second hand tuxedo suits
To look your very best to be forgotten
When dead end streets are named after you
Only you will remember if you existed or not
Long after the holes on the tired soles
Of your shoes are available to scholars
Of obsolete libraries in neighborhood
Of abandon frame of mind and broken hearted
Wine bottles waiting to be congratulated
When by coincidence we don't meet again
To play hide and seek with ancient winos
Of the subconscious who fall off mental
Bar stools on psychosomatic flying saucers
Destine for the society of sleepless nights
On the rooftops of make believe buildings
Where the intoxicated Poet in residence
Needs a haircut and a shave and a bath
To look his best when he deliberately
Spills his drink on the host and hostess

Of closets where the world will end
To prove death has a good sense of humor
Hold your empty pockets up high and applaud
Though you were not born you will live
4 ever everytime someone loses their memory

TRAFFIC MISDIRECTOR

the greatest living poet
in new york city
was born in Puerto Rico
his name is Jorge Brandon
he is over 70 years old
he carries his metaphor
in brown shopping bags
inside steel shopping cart
he travels around with
on the streets of manhattan
he recites his poetry
to whoever listens
& when nobody is around
he recites to himself
he speaks the wisdom
of unforgotten palm trees
the vocabulary of coconuts
that wear overcoats
the traffic lights
of his poems function
without boring advice
from ac or dc current
book stores & libraries
are deprived of his vibes
to become familiar
with this immortal poet
you have to hang-out
on street corners
building stoops rooftops
fire escapes bars parks

subway train stations
bodegas botanicas
iglesias pawn shops
card games cock fights
funerals valencia bakery
hunts point palace
pool halls orchard beach
& cuchifrito stands
on the lower eastside
the admission is free
his presence is poetry

DRIVING WITHOUT A CAR

La ultima noche
Que you espend with yourself
You couldn't sleep
So you made a neighborhood weep
And became a legend to some
And a dead talented Puerto Rican
To others or otros depending on
How far you got in high school
Where you learned how to play
Musical instruments and write poetry
On days you were deliberately absent
From the classroom to educate
Yourself in social clubs with friends
Who had to drop out of school
To become successful in life
As proprietors of Bodegas on the moon
With Spanish juke boxes featuring
Records by Celso Vega & contemporaries
For the customers to dance to
While they shop for their groceries
And converse and have a drink
With El Bodeguero who died years ago
On the sidewalks of El Barrio
But since he never learned english
Had no problems coming back to life
To prove Bodegas are still alive
And well to assure college graduates
A Piraguero will always be a Piraguero
And don't ask for an explanation!
The newspaper said Celso hung

Or hanged himself with his own belt
The comic strips said he left town
To learn how to drive without a car
And that made much more sense
To me and Doctor Willie who always
Took off from school on his birthday
And attended classes on george
washington's aborted birthday
Because the teachers were absent
And it made learning possible
And we could listen to music
While learning how to fly airplanes
Back to where we understand
What La Ultima Noche means

NO PARKING AT ANY TIME

The autumn leaves
Are extremely yellow
With orange blessings

Everybody walks
In slow motion
Balancing imaginary
Beer cans on their heads
Yawning with every step
They reluctantly take

A couple eating lunch
On a park bench scream
As they accidently
Eat each other

Dogs are heard barking
At an undertaker
Pushing a baby carriage
On his day off

Portable radios
The size of refrigerators
Are heard blasting
The eardrums of the wind

Blind gentlemen
Assist young ladies
With 20/20 vision
Across the street

A deaf mute tries
To sell a loose joint
To an unemployed priest

Teenagers bored
To death with school
Contemplate running
For President in
The next elections

Unpublished Poets dodge
Rocks the river throws
In their direction

I HATE TREES

In a subway train station
outside the jurisdiction
of my imagination I met
a sentimental elderly lady
who said these sad words
to me: I don't believe it
mistaken me for my brother
who was also my best friend
& now lives inside mirrors
you look into with your
eyes shut to see him again

when we were hanging out
together we traveled to
where darkness never ends
to handle special candles
& step a thousand years back
dressing monday in black
to converse about rainbows
visible only to those
destine to always fear
sleeping alone in the dark
to be able to be present
in every dream they had
about the fear & excitement
of never knowing what is
supposed to happen next

if i seem extremely upset
it's because IS no longer

difficult to write a poem
these broken hearted nights
when darkness occurs twice
& I think about mountains
My brother & I used to climb
in tenantment building days
of avoiding the correct time
when the name of the world
was Amsterdam avenue for us
always daydreaming we were
on a bus or a train to get
from one room to the next
& wait for real elevators
that we imagined were coming
to leave apartment nineteen
& ride down 5 antique floors
of history never to be lost
as long as baseball cards.
& bubblegum continue to
come to the rescue of kids
that never want to grow up
or to be interviewed for full
time jobs from 9to5 & beyond
with only one hour for lunch
not enough time to go home
& get turned on & forget our
freedom of movement has been
suspended & report back to
work late & punch the boss
instead of punching the time
card with our names mispelled
for raising hell at us for
arriving hours after the bell

rang ending the lunch break
from the factory of confusion
so we came to the conclusion

we needed the whole week
for lunch & weekends for work
on a poem or play or novel
that will make us famous in
all the rescue missions of
a foreign country called earth
where you must be on time
even if you have nowhere to go
or you will be reprimanded
by god & country & employer
& bearded shopping bag ladies
who looked & dressed weird
to scare us into adulthood
& they almost succeeded then

but thanks to our dead folks
we wrote our own ghost stories
that kept us from getting old
& denying the lies we once told
about the river not being deep
enough to make us lose sleep
to keep a private secret about
realizing we were down & out

Brother Poet & best friend
Correct me if I am right
you said let there be light
so we could stay out late
until all hours of the night
drinking & conversing about

the good old days not here yet
that we will never forget
as long as we laugh & laugh
while walking on the grass
that we were told to stay off
or be fined & be confined
to the house of detention

but we paid no attention
& didn't remove our hats
on the hottest day of summer
to hang out & lie about
being from San Francisco
to those who lie about being
from Nebraska or Alaska
because all roads of those
remarkable desolate times
of obscene Help Wanted Ads
led us to Manhattan State
where many years much later
we came to the conclusion
the doctors are the patients
at that mental institution
for casualties of romance
whose dreams will come true
if they give shock therapy
a chance to keep them bananas
on the times Square Shuttle
subway train to Puerto Rico
where trees are sociable
& drunken drivers live 4ever
this is one poem I never
wanted to write in my life
but darkness did occur twice

& wrong numbers didn't exist
the day his humor was missed
& it was him who was calling
on a phone that never rang
to inform us to weep & keep
dancing after the record ends
like back in the old days when
everybody owned a victrola
refrigerator & television set
except us NOT because we were
very poor BUT because we had
vivid imaginations to enjoy
the finer daydreams of life

and speak fluent chinese
on a russian roller coaster
with license plates from Mars
from the 1st day of september
until the last day of April
in the memory of monday night
an evening that we dedicated
to doing nothing at all right
to guess what time it wasn't
on the candles we had to light
to find the toys we lost when
there was no cost of living

his name was Dr. Willie
a free lance gynecologist
who took his humorous poems
more serious than we were
ever capable of taking ours
if the price was right
heads of state never invited

him to recite for them
because of his discontent
for dishonesty & politicians
they knew he will never
praise them with speeches
they prepared to enhance
their image in history books

he was 2 original to speak
like them or anybody else
who didn't owned a manual
typewriter that needed
a haircut & a shave & spare
change for a cup of coffee
a can of beer & cigarettes
he was too spontaneous
for the left & the right
& the space in the middle
nobody could follow his act
whose fantasies were facts
he could elaborately prove

he predicted world war 2
thirty years after it ended
& flew the first airplane
in a dream he once had
about the world going mad
& the good lord saying
daniel come forth & daniel
being the quick guy came
in 3rd & we heard ourselves
laughing in our deep sleep
in those housing projects
of daily bread & daily drugs

where we bugged our folks
to lie about being broke
& send us to school in
chauffeur driven limousines
like normal human beings
because we were convinced
that we were dignitaries
& we knew that if we died
sooner or later we would
escape from the cemetery

nickle bags were half ounces
in those adventures of being
young enough to hide with
wine bottles under umbrellas
because it was really raining
& we were never complaining
but laughing extremely loud
as we flipped a coin to decide
who will be the lst one to die

heads you cry at my funeral
tails I will faint at yours

we both wished we had lost
but somebody had to win
because because because
it can never ever be a draw
once that coin goes up
down again it has to fall
until it hits the sidewalks
of picture post cards
of memories in black & white
on sunday afternoon picnic

on roof top of buildings
prematurely demolished
to keep the wise disorganized
until the final demised
of their dignity & integrity

the coin kept falling
after it had hit the ground
until it landed on the stoop
Of 126 La Salle Street
where we will meet again
no longer afraid of the dark
on opposite sides of the mirror
we used to comb our hair in
to win baseball games in parks
that have been converted
into urban battlefields for
teenagers with drinking problems
& homeless senior citizens

the past was your future
you never ran away from home
you were determined to stay
even after all the neighbors
had moved out or passed away
your childhood days had no end

old buildings will be new again
& there will be light to see
& there will be running water
& it will be a great society
it was a dark monday night
& everything was alright
it was raining agua florida

in that room reserved for
lit candles A red rose & songs
from El Trio Los Panchos

Dr. Willie Joe Carmen & I
drank and sang and laughed
& ate southern fried chicken
from Faye Cooper's kitchen
& badmouthed everybody who
wasn't superstitious enough
to celebrate with us & them
who were present & absent from
the correct day of the week

without using words to speak
or the floor to keep moving
forward & backwards endlessly
we had a far out conversation
in a language from no nation
on the face of this planet
until a toy telephone rang
& we applauded our Madama
looking fine on the other line
of this blind communication

it was a darker monday night
when the poem I dreaded to write
wrote itself with my eyes shut
& my head buried in my hands
trying hard not to understand
why man can only walk thru walls
at the end of the person they
were born to be for a brief
moment in the history of life

it was darker than darkness
on that endless monday night
Dr. Willie became out of sight

& I remained here on earth
for fear of upsetting my wife
BUT POETS are not suppose
to get married he said to me
that I said to him years ago
& I had to agree that I was
no longer practicing whatever
I did or didn't preached
so he lost sleep by himself
& I never saw my friend again
because now when I am awake
he is asleep & only wakes up
in dreams I have about him

O I hate trees I swear I do
death wasn't suppose to happen
to someone as poetic as you
crazy enough to live forever
with your universal sense
of humor that was fantastic
Martians also laughed when
you got drunk and told jokes
even tho they spoke no spanish
or broken hearted English

that damn tree was to blame
for making you forget what
your name & home address was
It should have not been there
at 6 o'clock in the morning

when people who party all
night long are busy speeding
in the dead wrong direction
of their better judgment

to forget that you didn't
die alone is to forget
that you didn't die at all
There was also Maria and
Maria and Mario or Maria
and Mario and Maria or
Mario and Maria and Maria
who was 7 months pregnant
under the influence of
thunderbird or bacardi rum
I dedicate this eulogy
that you wrote to them too
whose real names & dreams
& ambitions I never knew

give them my best regards
in the night clubs of the sky
they will never be forgotten
by those who remember they died

keep up the fun & laughter
in the mysterious hereafter
the motorcycle gang will
continue to get high & never
forgive that goddamn tree
that interrupted your poetry
It had no business being
awake at the break of dawn

to end your memories of now
to end your memories of now

No, I will never learn how
to admit you reached the sky
your demise was never on
my agenda because our folks
said we will live forever
& of course we believed them
they had no reason to lie
that means you have not died
you are still hanging out
there is nothing to cry about
disregard this eulogy doc
I will turn back the clock

& tell John you are not gone
there is still reason
to be afraid of the dark
& tell Juan the show continues
is the audience that ends
& converted to empty seats
& tell Joe it isn't so
there is still time to meet
and greet the flames of
new candles on monday night
& tell Frank our minds just
went blank for the time being
& tell Ernesto to erase it
from his manifesto of reality
& agree with Sam that seeing
is seeing & not believing
& remind Papoleto residing

In the mental West Coast
to reprimand his holy ghost
for sleeping on the job while
a poet was being deprived
of the metaphor of being alive

Dr. Willie Latin Insomniac
thank you for making us .laugh
& thank you for making us cry
none of us will ever forget
this was the only way for you
to return To Ponce Puerto Rico
to meet the princess you love
in the forest of total silence
where whispers of oceans are
heard confessing word for word
Poet you have eternal blessings
in this story & glory of art
that never ends but starts anew
after life on earth is thru
& peace is familiar with you
& peace is familiar with you

II

Many times I have wept
Many times I have not slept
Many times I have dranked
Many times my mind has gone blank
Thinking deeply about
The last night you went out
And decided to never return
At last you had finally learned
How to stop wearing your hat

And feel important about that
And feel important about that

More than once before a second
Is completed I have thought about
The holy person you have become
By moving your spirit out of your body
In the most undressed time of existence
To find the mirror that will memorize
The end of time & beginning of eternity
When we exchange identity with the wind

More than once I have called you
When I have been totally speechless
And waited impatiently for your reply
And only heard the sound of silence
And the darkness that now prohibits
Daylight from getting personal with you
And yes it left me depressed my friend
And I walked around in endless circles
And made plans to eulogize myself
Though it was you who came to an end
I felt I was the one who had died

III

I want to communicate with you
Now more than ever than before
I don't care if I am accused
Of talking to myself in public
I don't care if I am committed
I don't care if I never get released
I want to communicate with you
In whatever language you speak now

I will stop thinking to learn it
I will forget everything I know
I will not answer if I hear my name
Called by those outside of walls
You and I still have to converse
No one was supposed to die first

I want to communicate with you
I will learn how to light candles
With my fingertips and become
Silent enough to impersonate you
In that room where you last saw
The person that will always be you

I don't care if grown ups laugh
I don't care if children get scared
Or if my peers think I am weird
And out of touch with their reality
Because as far as I am concerned
Their facts have nothing to do with me
I believe in the total resurrection
Of best friends to get drunk again

Everyone says you have passed away
Everyone except your next poems
That proves we can still hang out
And recite with the absence of light
And pass a bottle of rum around
Everybody but you has left town
I don't care who says it isn't true

I want to communicate with you
To prove the last letter isn't zzzz
Feel free to mentally disturb me

If it takes insanity to communicate
With you who will always be great
I have no other ambition my friend
there is no end to the conversation
We started when flying was easy
And dying was absolutely impossible
For companions like us to ever do

I want to communicate with you
Doctor Willie Count Guillermo
Ralph Gonzales and what other names
Claim the fame of your personality
Never false but eternally true
In ballfields where nothing is real
In bars where important we are
On street corners and hallways
Where we harmonized & fantasized
About becoming Rock N Roll Singers
To make all our dreams come true

I want to communicate with you
I want to communicate with you
To sing do do do doo oo ooo again
because nothing ends not even the end
you will always be my brother
you will always be my best friend

TO GET DRUNK YOU HAVE TO DRINK

Unseen faces keep appearing
In the evening of the sky
No one saw what they were hearing
Unseen faces keep appearing
Those who were not born were fearing
That they too will someday dy
Unseen faces keep appearing
In the evening of the sky

There was never no tomorrow
It was all about today
When you and the Doctor quarrels
There was never no tomorrow
Return all the dreams you borrowed
From remote control highways
There was never no tomorrow
It was all about today

This planet is still unknown
Though it may seem very clear
Mysteries are all we own
This planet is still unknown
Everyone alive stays stone
Until it is time to disappear
This planet is still unknown
Though it may seem very clear

Start driving without a car
All the lights are turning red
If you want to get real far
Start driving without a car

Move by staying where you are
The steering wheel is in your head
Start driving without a car
All the lights are turning red

Inside darkness there is light
Inside water there is fire
Black magic is out of sight
Inside darkness there is light
Turning left is turning right
Coming down is getting higher
Inside darkness there is light
Inside water there is fire

Blue was never really blue
Pink was never really pink
Somebody was fooling you
Blue was never really blue
What is false is really true
To get drunk you have to drink
Blue was never really blue
Pink was never really pink

OUT OF
ORDER

TELEPHONE BOOTH

numero zero

Is a collection of anti prose
conversations in non alphabetic
impromptu numerical free verse disorder
that began one night I couldn't sleep
and had no choice but to wake up
staring out the window at myself
desperately attempting to make
a social call at ungodly hour of nite
because solitude had stabbed me in
the back and I bled loneliness
which got worse every time I lost
a quarter trying to end a conversation
on the phone which all seem to be
out of order so with my last quarter
I decided if it was out of order
or not I was going to start a conver
sation regardless and yes it was
out of order and I had a long
interesting conversation with no one!

TELEPHONE BOOTH

number 801

no, of cause not,
I will not look at a man
the same way I look
at a woman, there is a difference
one makes me very horny
and the other one does not,
but I will not tell you
which one, if you want
that information you will
have to take off your clothes

TELEPHONE BOOTH

number 905½

woke up this morning
feeling excellent,
picked up the telephone
dialed the number of
my equal opportunity employer
to inform him I will not
be into work today
Are you feeling sick?
the boss asked me
No Sir I replied:
I am feeling too good
to report to work today,
if I feel sick tomorrow
I will come in early

TELEPHONE BOOTH
number 339 ½

daydreaming
about darkness
my imagination
faints inside
lost volume
of unwritten
poetry (the clothes
that follow
my skin around
escape from
the empty space
I am wearing)
the halfmoon
doesn't mind my
indecent exposure
(neon signs
fall from my
head) in fast
and slow motion

TELEPHONE BOOTH

number 678

there is a rumor
that a Oppenheimer
Ana Oppenheimer
is really a river
that hides the moon
to protect it from
renegades of magic
in restless nights
of greater darkness
where a religion
called love began
to investigate time
before time existed
in a forest of eyes
staring into space
reserved for candles
to be lit by Ana
dark good news lady
of everlasting hills
filled with miracles
of oral simplicity

TELEPHONE BOOTH

number 12345

chico tito & tico
have never been
to Puerto Rico
but wear straw hats
play dominoes
drink cerveza fria
at cuchifrito stand
visit Botanicas
instead of shrinks
are non violent
until the're ordered
to remove straw hat
then volcanoes rebel
against daylight
& heaven surrenders
the ticket to hell

TELEPHONE BOOTH
number 65478

Estebita was so black
that magic had no choice
but to believe in him
Under the influence
of rum and agua florida
he walked thru walls
in the town of Belgica
across the street from
the republic of Cangrejo
sugar cane district of
eternal sun blessings
rooster inspired society
of everlasting fiction
Estebita was so human
Heaven came to him when
he stopped playing dominoes

TELEPHONE BOOTH

number 36421483

I don't have to drink
to tell you I love you
I have to drink after
I tell you I love you

TELEPHONE BOOTH

numbers 8976

with the best of intent
this phone cell documents
all the imaginary urban
post operation boost strap
witchcraft immigrants from
the westside & the eastside
Botanicas of Spanish Harlem
whose dignity was saved by
Be Bop Acapela Nationalism
in the oral tradition of
the hippest Freedom Fighter
outside english text books
Don Pedro Albizu Campos!
who said and keeps repeating:
To take our Country You
    Have to take our
      LIFE

TELEPHONE BOOTH

number 48

cemeteries to the right
cemeteries to the left
cemeteries in front of you
cemeteries in back of you
miles and miles and miles
of speechless tombstones
its impossible to get a hardon
when you are in long island

TELEPHONE BOOTH
number 9879

my folks have
walked on the moon
before space ships
were marketable
they exchanged original
overproofed rum
with the indigenous
inhabitants of the moon
for manual typewriters
to leave under christmas
trees and hopefully
one of their children
will grow up to save
the oral tradition
of not punctuating

TELEPHONE BOOTH

number 67409

i am not against
who i am against
i am against who
i am not against

TELEPHONE BOOTH

number 1359

so lets go home
so we can get
into an argument
so you can throw me
out of your house
so I can continue
working on that
endless epic poem
about loneliness

TELEPHONE BOOTH
number 35465

it was a castle
not a ghetto,
we were dignitaries
not immigrants,
we stayed on the moon
& only came down
to go to the bodega
for more cafe bustelo

TELEPHONE BOOTH
number 83½

the magic of
writing poetry
is not knowing
how to do it
right or wrong!

TELEPHONE BOOTH
number 1533130

earlier than the early
wind blows uninterrupted
outside all the windows
on canal street with
a lit flashlight I locate
some marijuana to roll
a reefer quickly & lite
UP inhaling in slow motion
begin remembering nada

TELEPHONE BOOTH

number 143503001

the night
doesn't end
until I complete
a poem that will
never be completed

TELEPHONE BOOTH
number 7783

witchcraft orgasm
purple green scene of
passionate knives flying
in you outer direction
blah blah blah quote
unquote til further notice
dead nurse has nice ass
as long as we don't run
out of grass & good rum
to keep the message from
getting across directly

TELEPHONE BOOTH

number 309

Professor Frank Pietri
the 3rd – secretary of state
of mind of the Latin insomniacs
motorcycle club without motor
cycles – bought us our first
futuristic pint of thunderbird
wine – for 60 cents collected
from all 13 members of the cubs
(which meant Cute Urban Boys)
we all had exciting disgusting
hangovers the following morning!

TELEPHONE BOOTH

number 500

do not love me
like you
love your brother
unless you
and your brother
are lovers
I refuse to pretend
I only want you
for a friend,
the conversation
cannot start
until we see
each other clearly
in the darkest
second of silence

TELEPHONE BOOTH
number 484

one late afternoon
many autumn hangUps ago
strange bull dozers
flattened out the wind
state of shock children
jump out of windows
to land on the last
playground about to be
converted into memories,
gun shots are heard
along with ambulance
siren speeding around
in circles going nowhere,
I take time out from
being scared to wonder
what does this have to do
with Puerto Ricans?

TELEPHONE BOOTH
number 579½

visiting a doctor
at Bellevue Hospital
equal opportunity
mental institution
armed with fig newtons
45 rpm record memory
poems I wrote
that he experienced
& some wine
hidden in hero sandwich
to take us back to
those magical hallways
of tenement destiny
where to harmonize was
our only ambition in
the land of acapela
& yes we were famous
& broke as all hell
when the visit ended
nurse told him 2 leave

TELEPHONE BOOTH

number 436

split seconds
of uncontaminated originality
flashing briefly through
endless mental corridor
towards garden of amnesia
to remember that if
the united states hadn't invaded
Puerto Rico in eighteen 98
we will still be able to land
on the moon spontaneously
& be back in time for supper!

TELEPHONE BOOTH

number 23

you who opened the eyes
of the river without rehearsing,
you who made a very important
contribution to the vocabulary
of the wind whose complexion is perfection,
you who introduce mountains and
rainbows to the memory of time & space,
you who went beyond light and darkness
to talk without the assistance of words,
you who closed your eyes to see
from your womb came the earth & the sky
your breast is the inception of love
when your were born cemeteries dropped dead,
those who know how to read and write
have nothing to say to you anymore,
they think I am talking to myself
they do not know that just the clothes
you wore were buried that day
with the flavor of the night in the air,
embrace my breath whenever you please,
later for them lets keep talking forever
is my tum to give birth to you new
let me know after what flower
you want to be named

TELEPHONE BOOTH
number 7652907

if I could
I would decline
the offer of
peace of mind
& wipe windshields
of automobiles
for a living
but because I am
who I am they
are who they are!

TELEPHONE BOOTH
number 356807

because I do not
want to make
future generations
lose sleep I
will do my very best
not to influence
anyone regardless
of what a nice ass
they seem to have

TELEPHONE BOOTH

number 203½

in times that were never
and never again will be
regardless of regardless
on the last day of history
when all has been said
do not mourn the losers
mourn the ones who have won

TELEPHONE BOOTH

number 376507

abuelo
means mechanic
in some circles
in other circles
it means manic messiah
on the roller coaster
at Coney Islandless
where he wore his best
domingo attire higher
than the parachute
to attend a wedding
as soon as he found out
who is getting divorce

TELEPHONE BOOTH

number maybe 58

i am
madly in love
with somebody
who has the most
wonderful ness
personality ness
that anybody
will want to meet
& live with
until light
becomes obsolete
& the bones
embrace darkness
& somebody has to
put up the money
to escort
the romance
below the surface
because sooner
or later you
or your love
will become
hazardous
to your health

TELEPHONE BOOTH
number 658003

yesterday is today
in a town in Ponce
where the folks are
looking for supernatural
mangoes – to feed the wind
a taste of history
that cannot be erased
with imposed assimilation
from military occupation
& modification education
because 4 your information
a nation is a nation
regardless of size-zation
not a place for vacation
for forces of occupation
grow your own mangoes
in microwave ovens –!
warn those magic jibaros
today from centuries ago

TELEPHONE BOOTH
number 766½

Jorge Brandon
is a friend of mine
has invaded
the u.s.a. many times
for messing with
talking coconut
which he promised
to give to his palm trees
for a wedding gift

TELEPHONE BOOTH

number 0854650

with the best of intent
this phone call documents
Felix Cortez who once said
I have to write about
Puerto Ricans while walking
up or down Broadway's upper
west side troubled dreams
& I agreed & disagreed be
cause what comes out of me
is about Puerto Ricans even
if is about something else
& the following evening
I wrote a long poem called
The Puerto Rican Obituary —
that was twenty years ago
in the autumn of nineteen 68
when revolution was great
& parking meters were diag
nosed as being schizophrenic

TELEPHONE BOOTH

number 568

it's less
complicated
to perform
open heart surgery
with needle & thread
than to complete
a poem that doesn't
begin or end
in the middle

TELEPHONE BOOTH

number 54301

minority poets
who write about
minority issues
such as the sea
the wind & the ocean
& hidden valley
leading to shadows
of liberated verse
cannot be referred to
as mental midgets
bitter & very hurt
but as pioneers
of independence –

TELEPHONE BOOTH
number 658¼

Chalo isn't a republican
or registered democrat
his policies are candles
he handles quite well —
by predicting the past
he sees into the future

TELEPHONE BOOTH

number 8986987

with the best of intent
this phone call documents
washington square park
pedestrians from all parts
of the anti art republic
of fuck you national anthem
one goddam nation under
creative disorder for all
who quit full time jobs
to screw the constitution
of wherever they are from
& come to dig the street
entertainers going crazy
in between lost manuscripts
of masterpieces of holy shit
that spits truth in saliva
on the bohemian pavement

TELEPHONE BOOTH

number 659

freedom IS
a four letter word
with a few extra
letters attached
to keep the conver
sation from ending

TELEPHONE BOOTH

number 654875

with the best of intent
this phone call documents
Miguel Algarin
Miguel Piñero
& Lucky Cienfuegos
of Nuyorican phenomena
liberated urban base verse
from all over the world
of their vivid imaginations
from the nation of Boriquen
& the Lower East Side
6th street Poet's Cafe
where La Noche Nunca ends

TELEPHONE BOOTH
number 0575½

there is a poem missing
which I don't know
where I misplaced it
there is a missing poem
which the poem doesn't
know where it misplaced
itself missing which
I don't know where
there is a poem missing
which where I misplaced
I don't know & neither
does the missing poem
the poem and I misplaced

TELEPHONE BOOTH
number 92345

all my friends are dead
or alive anticipating dying
in the very near future —
don't answer my doorbell
anymore — the battle was lost
in the war to live for ever
don't take it personal and
stop talking to me because
all poems cannot be about
pleasant days in the dark
to leave our mistakes uncor
rected — along with sunshine
there has to be hangovers

TELEPHONE BOOTH

number 797301

there is something
going on between us
we turn each other on
in more ways than 13
the following morning
there is nothing
going on between us
we turn each other off
in more ways than 31
that means we know a lot
& nothing at all about
how this conversation
starts & ends & starts

TELEPHONE BOOTH
number 158715

if you haven't had
a nervous breakdown
you haven't written
a poem — you just
interfered with A
blank page minding
its own business

TELEPHONE BOOTH
number 0671

poetry means
to wake up
every day and
make many mistakes
until it's time
to be unable to sleep
and leave mistakes
uncorrected in dreams
of being almost perfect

TELEPHONE BOOTH

number 75753

a state
without crisis
is a state
with art
because only
when you disagree
can there be
true creativity
in a society

TELEPHONE BOOTH

number 1599 or 1959

Rodrigo Ernesto
Manifesto Ortiz
is a immigrant
says the daily news
even tho he was
born in the united
states of amsterdam
avenue of memories
during acapela epoch
of Puerto Rican
nationalist making
history with the
guns the young
lords picked up
for a quick second!

TELEPHONE BOOTH
number ?????????????

I just changed my mind
about not doing anything
& continue doing nothing!
If you heard this before
don't feel significant
I hear it all the time
and never say anything
to anyone(not even)myself

TELEPHONE BOOTH

number HIJ

Get the hell
out of here
sit down and
make yourself
comfortable
I'll be back
as soon as I
am thru kick
ing you out
of this poem

TELEPHONE BOOTH

number 109 minus 19

I smoke grass
because I am not
allowed to walk
on the grass
if I was
allowed to walk
on the grass
I'll be able to
smoke grass
while walking
on the grass

TELEPHONE BOOTH

number 000001

From eternity
to here
quiet afternoon
across the street
where everyone
is missing
& only the blind
can read
traffic signs
that take
the mind off
your problems
when the light
changes & you
briefly have
freedom of move
     (ment)

TELEPHONE BOOTH
number 616

if I get up
to make the record
stop skipping
on the record player
I will certainly be
contradicting
everything I ever
said – about poetry

TELEPHONE BOOTH

number 8986586

with the best of intent
this phone call documents
Amiri Baraka who I met
as Leroi Jones in the library
shelf of Columbia University
contemporary poetry detention
section – & liberated his
books to introduce poems
to unemployed housing project
famous rock n roll singers
who earned minimum wages

TELEPHONE BOOTH

number 957

as we sweat drops of
the fullmoon into the eyes
of the night we invented
from the wind to give our
thoughts a complexion
that mountains & oceans &
sacred thunderstorms
will be very proud of,
we breathe into the conclusion
— In this world or the other
we will become lovers

TELEPHONE BOOTH

number 1

Special thanks to the typewriter
& the typewriter ribbon & number 2 pencils
& erasers & ko-rec-type & the table
that so graciously kept the typewriter
from falling on the floor & the chair
who did for me what the table did
for the typewriter – Without the effort
& endless cooperation of these personal
friends of mine it would have been impossible
to discontinue this endless conversation
that started in the winter or summer
or autumn or springtime of the year 1971
while losing a dime trying to call somebody
on a public telephone that was out of order
And Sam Diaz the Poet from
the desert of a Brooklyn Basement
apartment who years later demystified
high technology through poetry begat
by manual typewriter enabling
the manuscript to surface from the
Endless Blank page it took to keep out of order
and be read at your own risk or not at all!!!

EL
PARTY
CONTINUES

ORCHARD BEACH

It was Summertime again
& the living wasn't easy
For no longer recent
In category of immigrant,
Attending college at last

In a society bias to
Equal opportunity for us
Who met at the beach
In the month of sunday
To take the day off from
Phone bills and politics

To look forward to seeing
Dylcia Pagan in the sand
On A Puerto Rican blanket
With enough room for an
Entire Island to relax
At Orchard beach republic

By not so beautiful sea
To swim back to Borinquen
When the summer was over
And continue enjoying
The impeccable climate
Under the full time sun

That only shines partime
On certain occasions
In East Harlem experience
Where we all overslept

At one time or the other
Many summer meries ago
Where winter is control
Of the body & mind (but)
Definitely not the soul

We made the best out of
Limited pleasant weather
At Orchard Beach scene
Of non american dream
Where a Latin breeze
Speaks fluent Spanglish

& though there are no
Tropical palm trees aqui
Every now & then coconuts
Fall down from the sky
Proving que paradise also
Speaks with an accent:

I would say and Dylcia
Will tell me to shut up
And enjoy myself for
A change of attitude
Towards the near future
That kept wetting our feet

Where the heat begins
To remind us of a time
When we wouldn't have
To be meeting this way

Today or maybe tomorrow
Where the beach is always

Within walking distance
Of el simpatico sunshine
Amante of the weather
Forever within us (amen
For some and Vaya for
Others) as entire body
Becomes free of anxiety

Endeared by undercurrent
Of another time & place
In the rain of a forest
Of magic that never ends
& once again my friend
Tells me to shut up and
Enjoy myself for a change!

This is Orchard Beach
Not Brooklyn college
Where we first met at
Political poetry recital
Dylcia had arranged to
Take me out of the closet
Of poets at an early age

And it was successful
Because it was serious
As serious as the beach
Was on that summer day
About having a nice time
And not rhyme but swim
And take in the sun
Before the winter comes
Which is what everyone
Came to the beach to do

Not just listen to you
You listen to them too
Congueros are poets also
Pleneros are philosophers
Of guaguanco awareness!
Tho la vida isn't easy
We can still jump higher
Than impossible dreams
To follow our ambition
Of total independence
In & out of imagination
Of the nation we are

On this temporary beach
Of this everlasting day
In the memory of friends
Here then and here now

As otro can of cerbeza
Fria is given to poet
To hear his next poem
And this time Dee says:

If he's not busy reciting
He is busy drinking…
And the beer can laughed
Along with the crowd
We had gradually become
At Orchard Beach where
We knew and cared about
Each other's well being
Even if some of us didn't
Know how to dance mambo!

I guess we had a crush
On Dylcia Pagan back then
For keeping us together
At the beach or her
Brownstone Apartment
In Spanish Harlem across
The street from church
That changed our lives
Not through religion
But through politics

In the oral tradition
Of the poetry recitied
During a certain time
When we all got to heaven
Without leaving El Barrio
And Dee became the poet
We wrote about becoming
Without just thinking
About herself but about
Every single one of us

Who was at Orchard Beach
That sentimental summer
Or somewhere else to
Enjoy climate of comfort
Getting together brings
For people who can dance
With or without music

Where El Bronx almost ends
If you don't know how
To swim to keep friends

From becoming strangers
On pleasant memory beach
In the summer of 1971
The year that I became
An official sad orphan
Which many there were
& enjoying themselves too

Not just wondering why
Do Fools Fall In Love?
Or wondering why did
Frankie Lyman and the
Teenagers didn't get rich
After becoming famous?

Dee the mother figure
Made a point of stating
While I was busy dating
Someone in my other mind
Who didn't mind if I was
Depressed most of the time
Until the autumn of 1973
When everyone but the
Foot prints on the beach
Had gone home to wonder
Where did the summer go?

To look for our dreams
Of someday never again
Leaving tropical beach
Within walking distance
From el sacred bedroom
We wake up the morning
In a society of free

Cafe con leche for all

Which isn't impossible
If the Ochard Beach
You are refering to
Has Left New York City
To where we were born
To not only just have
Puerto Rico en el corazon
But everwhere you look
And everywhere you swim
To meet each other again
Where summer never ends

Don't forget el aquacate
And el queso blanco too
Con lettuce & tomates
Now that we are all
Vegetarian who only eat
Pasteles at the annual
Puerto Rican Day Parade

The only day Ochard Beach
Speaks without an accent
Until the parade ends
And dark clouds return
To dreams of freedom
Of movement & expression
Regardless of how pleasant
We thought the weather
Was forcasted as being
In the summertime when Dee
Was always good looking

At Ochard beach reminding
Artist and intellectual
And parapsychologist too
From El Barrio to do
Something revolutionary
Like enjoy themselves
For a change and maybe
They will learn how to
Dance el mambo at last

And not have to wait
For a slow bolero to ask
Someone out to dance
& she'll politely reply
I only dance salsa music!

And instead of learning
How to dance the way
The future knows how to
You left the dance before
The music had ended
To continue writing
The poem already written
That bought us together
Where summer is endless
And the living is easy
If you work very hard

THE PARTY CONTINUES
For Eduardo Figueroa

Welcome to
The 21st century
The nineties are over
The eighties never came!
You can now decide
to stop being occupied
for the last time once again—
How were you feeling back then?
Great! You can now feel greater
It's never too late
To make plans for the past
If the future is to have a present!

On your next sightseeing tour
Through space stay down to earth
For best results of what you
Were looking for and didn't find
Because it was all in your mind
The only place you didn't look
For that endangered species
In the invaded memory of 1898!
Puerto Rico was never far away
New York City is the foreign
Country outside the imagination—

I know you heard this before
But the airplane really didn't
Take off! So remove the OverCoat
The scarf and the wool gloves
And put on supernatural straw hats

And teach yourself how to dance
The way your ancestors knew how!
Their house is still your house
Their eyes are still your eyes
Their hands are still your hands

The airplane stayed behind
New York is a state of mind!

AND WHERE DID WE GO
EVERYWHERE AND BEYOND ELSEWHERE!

There are Puerto Ricans on the moon
They were selling Piraguas there
Long before the 1st astronauts
Lied about walking on the moon!
Space Bodegas are not uncommon!
They stay open all night long
To celebrate the 365 holidays
On the calender of Puerto Ricans
Who can walk through walls
To discover that they were
Not only born in Puerto Rico:

But everywhere else there are people
Who like to have a nice time
Because the mind is a terrible
Thing that is absolutely brilliant
Which makes us all remarkable
And substantiates the fact
That Einstein was also Puerto Rican

By saying Free Puerto Rico
You are saying Free the Universe

Long live the Spirit Republic
At night in the eyes of daylight
For liberty justice & infinity
For all who don't need license
Or registration or passport
To enter the imagination & stay
Until you can honestly say
You are born in a different
Country everyday of your life!

You did nothing wrong
You did everything right

In the daytime you said
GooooooooooooD Night!
That qualifies you to be free
If you want to be free!

GOD BLESS EVERYBODY!
NOT JUST AMERICA OR AMERICO!

Later for plebiscites
You were born with the right
To determine your destiny
And say let there be light
In the eyes of the night
Even if you must kick ass
To walk on your own grass
Kick ass without the use
Of deadly weapons that destroy
The losers and the winners
The pen will always be
Mightier than the sword

Detrimental to immortality—

If we don't kill anyone
We can all live forever
To keep the party going
Into the century after the next
And the one after that one
Until we all meet again
In the beginning not the end
To do what we do best
& that is to contemplate success
Through universal harmony
At the Puerto Rican Embassy
Where you don't have to be
Puerto Rican To Be Puerto Rican
or any other nationality!

And oh yes we can see
Ourselves inside of everybody!
From sea to shinning Sea!

    (Senor)
    From Viejo San Juan
    to modern Spanish Harlem
    From Rio Piedras
    to the South Bronx

    From Santurce to
    Brooklyn and Queens
    And Staten Island too
    from Fajardo
    to Philadelfia
    From Bayamon to Boston
    from Coabey to Conneticut

from Arecibo to New Jersey
from Mayaguez
to New Hampshire
from Ponce to Maine
also familiar with
La plena and the
late eternal Elena
who knew for a fact
that there is no
Such thing as
A Puerto Rican American
because we never
melted America
invaded us on
the 25 of July today
100 years ago

LOVE
POEMS
TO MY
SURREALIST
GYPSY

HER SIMPLICITY IS HER MYSTERY

There is no danger of her
living forever (she will die
Of natural causes one night
& be reborn the next morning)

She wasn't created in one day
It took forever to meet her.
Many walls had to be stared at
waiting for a poem to occur

Until the unexpected moment
of an unforgettable feeling
In the journey of searching
for someone to love arrived

And I survived to document
the experience late at night
with a beginning & no ending
memorizing a silent sunflower

PUERTO RICAN HYSTORY BLUES

The clouds we at night become
will always be wide awake
on the tropical dance floor
to keep Boleros on the map
of the hometown we never saw

Sorry to inform the moon
there's nothing else on my mind
but thoughts of the last time
my spirit left your Island

To sooner or later find out
where darkness spends the night
not allowing us to sleep a wink
until our number is unlisted
and our address doesn't exist

Only then will we remember
where did the romance go
now that the marriage is legal
and the love is experimental

ODE TO WITCH LIBERTY

Rooster feathers replace the wings
Of fallen angels from Purgatory
To make them look young once again
Ready to crow at the break of dawn
And reverse the night into daylight
After the external nocturnal flight
Into the final feelings of her arms
That turns love on and off and on
Until eternity is within reach of
A never to be forgotten moment
And evidence of after life passion
Materializes before the naked eye!—
Beware! She is wise & unpredictable
Holds you tight to keep you loose,
Her heart tells the truth & nothing
But! Until the honeymoon is over
And you will never again be sober
Or drink from the same strange river
Of times that misplaced your vanity
And left you far away from yourself
To dance with a human space race
Among the bright and darker lights
Of her perfumed conceptual bedroom
Where lit candles handle darkness
Extremely well when there are no lies
To tell the comfort death receives
Where the missing persons loiter
Talking absentmindedly to themselves
Until a ripe coconut from a palm tree

They no longer remember climbing
Drops on the center of the skull
And they briefly feel witch liberty
Smiling as the spirit leaves the body
From one dead vagrant to new hobo
Infant tender & mild & wild & destined
To misplace many things in life
Because she will never be the wife
Of he or anybody who tries to modify
Her down to earth psychic powers—
And she only accepts frozen flowers
From gardens where it snows constantly,
Oh it is there her fires come from
To decorate her soul with dark secrets
From flames that forget your name
As you remember who you never were
Inside thoughts of frogs and lizards
That chased a snake off the roof
And it fell into a lake of ironic soup
That cures and kills you for sure
To keep your dreams inside your head
So that they may never have to end
And you can assume Witch Liberty
And you are an inseparable extension
Of the same Island reserved 4 silence
As long as you pledge high allegiance
To your imagination—she will follow
To make you feel like a real king
Destined to become her slave any day
As fact & fantasy becomes the same
& you better not mention her name
While she is occupied meditating
Or she will surely drive you insane
& chase you onto a midair collision

With unidentifiable flying objects,
And you will never again be able
To make another round table rise—
With Liberty just wants the world
for a friend NOT overprotective lover
Companion circus ring leader hermit
In old clothes compatible to Zen—
She fell off the highest wire once
Upon a few mundane misunderstandings
About who said Let there be light!
Her heart cannot be broken twice
So Poet become your own fatal wife
If what you fear most is insecurity!
She is sure and unsure of everything
Now that she knows where the wind
Goes when it doesn't blow in the air,
If you stare She will be there
To let you watch her comb her hair
At twilight time in all her thoughts
Of how the world ended a long time ago
Because no one alive believed in magic
And so the sun had no reason to rise
Inside the eyes of sleepy children—
Rain & thunder & occasional lightning
Accompanied the dilemma of being
Realistic as head falls off shoulder
And is never seen or heard from again
At the end of the endless sexy pause
In a nightmare about happy endings—
We are only pretending—Aren't we?
Hell No! Heaven yes! Replies Witch
Of Liberty for all who are present
The following amnesia induced morning
While it's still dark enough to see

And you have to go and keep coming
Til you meet again to propose love
& marriage & stability & boredom
& disappointment til death survives
The crisis in a divorce from life
For making her your personal wife
Without ever becoming her friend—
And once again she will refuse to be
The bottom of your missing deep blue
Spirit sea of sacred contradictions
That deliver you not from evil ever
So that you may never be able to
Imagine a short cut to paradise
At the entrance of her third eye
The eye that sees everything clear
And knows nothing about anything
Until all the lights are turned off

LOOSE
POEMS

LETTER FROM A VIETNAM VET

Dear Mom,

Today I got turned on
To grass in Vietnam
Please do not get alarmed
All my problems are gone
I want to do no harm
To no one in Vietnam
Please do not get alarmed
And read the 23rd Psalm
Because I got turned on
To grass in Vietnam
Where people talk on and on
With faces that are calmed
Why should we do them harm
Dropping down deadly bombs
Let's get out of Vietnam
Most of the children are gone
And will never get turned on
To grass that does no harm
And keeps you very calm
Please do not get alarmed
We have friends in Vietnam
Who never did us any harm
There is no reason to bomb
People with so much charm
They want to live on and on
In their beloved Vietnam
They also have school proms
Interrupted by our bombs
The G.I.s are all Johns

With minds completely gone
They only respect blondes
Everyone else they harm
These victims of false alarms
And prefabricated qualms
They are constipated Mom
And unable to go beyond
Propangander that turns them on
To the glory of dropping bombs
In countries like Vietnam
Many return home embalmed
That's why I got turned on
Please do not get alarmed
I am alright Dear Mom

THE LADY THINKS

The lady thinks
She is a shrink
Won't take a drink
She really stinks
Is on the brink
Of kitchen sinks
I tried to wink
She doesn't blink
The lady thinks
She is a shrink
And pink is pink
She really stinks
Give her a mink
But not a drink
She is a kink
Her mind went clink
She is no shrink
Ran out of ink
Is on the brink
Ice skates in rinks
And thinks & thinks
That pink is pink
She really stinks
Like a rat fink
I tried to wink
She doesn't blink
Cannot spell swink
Or slink or skink
Tick toc tic tink
She aint no shrink
Pink is not pink

Give her a drink
To blink & blink
Remove the mink
Her missing link
Don't really think
She is a shrink
But on the brink
Of kitchen sinks
Whatever that minks
or means in englink
Give her a drink
To blink & blink
Not sink & sink
When doctors wink
In her directchink
And do not think
She is a shrink
And pink is pink
Tic toc Tic tink
Tic toc Tic tink!

YES—I SWEAR TO THE STATUE OF MY LIBERTY . . .

That the abstract rear view mirror of
The faded olive purple crimson blue
Rear entrance to tunnel carnival
Was just pretending to put up a fight!
But as sure as the late Jesus Christ
Was able to turn the water into wine
I knew that everything will be fine
For this mad woman and madder man
In pursuit of milk&honey&quicksand—
At last there will be peace on earth
I kept repeating so it won't hurt
Feelings she never knew she possessed
As we confessed how obsessed we are
With the oral definition of decadence
To succeed in getting the message lost,
Because it wasn't a fucken rotten fruit
That got Adam and Eve expelled from
That exclusive suburban country club
In the garden of global oppressors
Of the past—the present—& future:
They were caught in the same position
That's censored on live television—
I whisper to my sister in the struggle
For deep eternal trouble all the dazed
Days of forever being a recent immigrant
From the half moon—soon to be fulled
As shock therapy abducts our destiny
At the moment of rebirth in newyorkcity
On a night incarcerated by our memory.

AFTER THE 7TH DRINK

staring at a lamp is also important

so let us shut our eyes and be repetitive

In the pursuit of ecstatic confusion

further away from the actual details

when something unrealistic pays a visit

for children & stray dogs to think about

uncivilized people that are special

becoming absolutely necessary to forget

for refusing to spell god correctly

& pledging allegiance to insubordination

never coming down to know how much higher

they are than their odd contemporaries

prisoners of daily despicable routines

who have never had the magic experience

of mispronouncing a word in english

AFTER THE 9TH DRINK

As I am about to begin & end
A conversation about the good old days
In an underground outdoor cafeteria—
A well dressed gentleman too short
To reach the top of the table
Steals an original volume of poetry
From a porter whose ambition in life
Is to someday be taken dead serious
& though the porter is articulate
He doesn't seem to understand that
Poets have time for nothing else
But the next poem & the next drink—
The porter feels insulted & starts
An argument with his vacuum cleaner
—the ceiling opens—wrinkled old men
Fall out head first dying of thirst—
I applaud & the porter gets pissed off
—the midget is destined for fame
As everyone forgets what they came here
To order—When peace is restored
A sudden rainstorm misquotes everyone!
I tell my company goodbye & open-up
My eyes to dream about something else
To be used for sub-titles in the bible—
God Almighty! Precious Mary! Lucifer Darling!

AFTER THE 11TH DRINK

God Almighty! Precious Mary! Lucifer Darling!
I call on all three of you entertainers
To my dark alley this early in the morning
To get permission from you GOD who works
In mysterious ways—& from your LUCIFER
Who only works on weekends & holidays—
Mary will heat up black coffee for us
Because she is still nine months pregnant
—O grant us permission to get very drunk
—O grant us permission to never sleep again
—O grant us permission to remain incoherent!
Mary get your feet out of the coffee pot
Is hot as hell & you will surely freeze
—O grant us a special grant to become
Derelict in residence when we get to heaven
To do speaking engagements in hell sober
Now that we are much older & less sensible
Praying with mix drinks in both hands
Accompany by the music of an obsolete band
Whose dead direction has amazing psychic powers
At all hours of the unpredictable night
When Mary begs me to kill her so she can live
A normal life—& I oblige by looking under
Her dress to locate my missing whereabouts
& walk out of the bar holy—staggering home
To the hereafter a poem has been completed

CONFESSIONS OF A TRANSISTOR RADIO

A night is heard beginning
A window is heard closing and closing
A cold breeze is heard changing colors
A pen is heard running out of ink
A blind man is heard seeing clearly
A sleep walker is heard whispering backward
A conversation is heard being dropped
A mother only wants her children for friends
And this could be the way the world ends

For the serious and the delirious
For the bright parasites of the night
The first to acknowledge the worst

In the technicolor hopes of cinemascope
Determined to blindfold the nightmares
Of tourists trembling on the windshields
Of premeditated automobile accidents
After fatal head-on collision ceremony
With the supernatural and the constipated
Casualties of vending machines & clinics
Where cash registers outnumber the patients
Demanding treatment for mental illness
After detecting gangrene in birthday cake
With flames on both ends of the candle
Below the surface of television antennas
Where saints faint forever shooting up
Obsolete newspaper articles about salvation
In the days of comic strips & skinless flicks
Shoved down childrens throats by folks
Whose hangovers were influenced by boredom

They held their dinner drinks upsidedown
To stain the clothes and not the brain
To look their best for the next commercial

When the meteorologist says:
We interrupt this program to inform you
That you & your friends have passed away!
It will be then it will be when
That without anticipating your next move
You will laugh as loud as you could
On the sidewalks of all the neighborhoods
You spent the nights alone in the arms
Of airmail stamps from childhood memories
When life was nice and you were bold
And the meals never got too cold to love
And you had the imagination to sin—
And this could be the way the world begins

(meanwhile back on the ground floor
after running out of buttons to press
you look down and start shouting
BUT I THOUGHT THIS WAS THE FIRST FLOOR!
how come I am still feeling very high?)

Bi-lingo umbrellas salesmen are seen
Jumping out of billboards in times square
Informing the general electric public:
Your next piece of ass will be your last!
Those who don't listen will be christened
With clorox & sniff embalming fluid at events
Commemorating their inability to function
After burning cigarette holes in their arms

Roses are red
Violets are blue
Is all that
Comes out of you
When you try
Explaining
To yourself
Why at the green
& not inbetween?
In the name of
Personal Saviors
Whose behavior
Blows your mind
In cheap wigs
& mini skirts
Turning on tricks
Behind the wheels
Of automobiles
In parking lots
Where every night
Is halloween
And the words
Of the song
Have been changed
To god bless
The Drag Queen.

And this is how wars are won
By Generals in bottomless uniforms
On their knees in sperm proof cathedrals
Wiping airplane glue off their lips
With pages from the Wall street journal
After receiving medals for corruption

To give masturbation a second chance
And save the nation's blind loyalty
For leaders who advocate self destruction

And now ladies and Gentlemen
We take great pleasure in introducing
To everyone here, someone who just left,
And won't be returning anytime soon,
He has finally accepted the fact
That he only wants himself for a friend
Because when dogs hear their master's bark
This is how the science fiction ends

The sky is the sky
It is listed as the sky
In the yellow pages
Where the messiah never ages
Whose only begotten son
Is the eternal Miss Subways
Who fell in love with
The third rail one day
And he was buried the next

This is all the information you need
To forget how to read & write & breakfast
Everytime you think you have woken up—are wide awake
In the name of topless dancers of both sexes
Who breast feed the missing persons
Lost forever inbetween a sandwich they ate.

The next time it rains do not seek
Asylum under an opened umbrella
But take time out to get very weird
And learn how to fuck again

Like you used to fuck way back when
Before you started losing your hair
& wearing bulletproof underwears
And your wife embraces the pillow
And you chew on the bedsheets
And this is how you both fall asleep
Every night of the anti-climactic week
To toss and turn on the front row
Of the last pornographic show they saw
On their first worst wedding anniversary
From the balcony of blank expression
Where nobody remembers who they are
And wives have eyes for plastic surgeons
And husbands flush themselves down toilets
Because their dicks have dropped dead
And the rent still has to be paid

They will grow up any second now
To become their own undertakers
After a lifetime of looking for eggs
In the meat where the vegetables weep

Sound & sight & darkness & light
Stops swimming inside their feelings
After they refused to accuse
Their illusions of first degree murder
They are to blame for the empty space
Present in their first and last names
Their hardons are casualties of seatbelts
Sold to them by popular politicians
Who promised to resurrect them
When ashes & dust & silence corrects them

(meanwhile back on the ground floor
after running out of buttons to press
you look down and start shouting
BUT I THOUGHT THIS WAS THE FIRST FLOOR!
how come I am still feeling very high?)

Ghosts picket the post office
They demand equal rights
They want to deliver the mail also
Just because they cannot be seen
Doesn't mean they cannot work
They too will get busted
If they are caught shop lifting.

You could have said FUCK-IT
Later for the mop and the bucket
And become a fulltime windshield wiper
On the streets of the Bowery
Wearing a discarded business suit
Found in the garbage cans of democracy,
But you grew up to become a man
Coming home from work without an erection
Looking for something edible to eat
Demanding your wife to scratch your feet
Who became a virgin 10 years after
You said I do & was unable to screw anymore
After nine out of ten medicine men
Pronounced you dead or alive or blind
For eating in the worst restaurants
Discussing a subject that was dropped
Long before the beginning of time
When decent funerals cost a dime or less
And everything you knew was guessed

Yes, you could have avoided death
But you didn't because those who expired
While you still sang in church choirs
Assured you it was still a nice day
The trees will not stay underground
Grass has infiltrated tall buildings
Plastic covers fail arithmetic again
Somebody you love will invite you
To the movies after the picture ends

GOD IS ALIVE
GOD IS ALIVE
The supermarkets inform
Those who got wet
Long before it started raining
LEAD US TO HIM
LEAD US TO HIM
They begged and pleaded
On their hands and knees
In the middle of a street
That was under the influence
Of heavy traffic
From all directions

But they did not know this
Because they knew how to read
And write and some have been taught
How to type 60 words per minute
They never reached the other side
Of the street where the doors
Of spring remain wide opened
And should your hair fall-out
The window you can jump after it
And there will be no bones brokened.

Now that you know this much less
About everything that was said
PULL OVER TO THE CURB IMMEDIATELY
The time has come to rehearse
For the performance you will not
Be invited to see now or later on

If you get there late
You will get there early
If you get there early
You will get there late
If you don't get there at all
You will get there on time:
Beware of sober people
And never trust a drunk
Before or after the ride—
There were just buttons to press
Not floors to get off on.
You will always feel very high
DO NOT ATTEMPT TO CRASH!
Your mission in life
Is to have a good laugh.

WHAT WAS THE DREAM ABOUT?

Approaching a river with nowhere to go
Rumors are that you have to take it slow
Inside your bedroom Roosters come and go
With good and bad news about your soul
Give them a standing ovation very soon bro
They will scare you but try not to shout
Tell us Eddie—What was the dream about?

Director of the real Puerto Rican Day Parade
Only in the imagination can one have it made
Burn down institutions to get the highest grade
For knowing it all nobody ever got paid
Your weapons are books not guns or switch blades
You have kept your mind off the negative route
Tell us Eddie—What was the dream about?

You thought you heard knocking at the front door
You looked in the mirror to find out the score
Wild horses stampede across the living room floor
You wake up inside a lonely hospital ward
Surrounded by casualties of an unexpected war
Of living forever you suddenly have doubts
Tell us Eddie—What was the dream about?

Has Laurel & Hardy returned from the dead?
Coquis can be heard from under your hospital bed
Santa Claus is A Capitalist Dressed in Red
There is something wrong with everyone's head
Who hides in between 2 slices of stale bread
The river is really wet There isn't a drought
Tell us Eddie—What was the dream about?

Is Frankie Lymon and the Teenagers back?
Are the doctors & nurses & aides high on crack?
Are they dealing from the bottom of the stack?
You are not one to stab yourself in the back
It has to be a dream in black&white & in black
Spring is here again Time to drink cold stouts
Tell us Eddie—What was the dream about?

There is no last stop for an artist to make
You have already won Give yourself a break
Do not write last wills behind common headaches
Your dreams can't come true if you aren't awake
Nobody is free at the bottom of a dry lake
Keep your faith in silence outside of your house
Tell us Eddie—What was the dream about?

The end is unreal beginnings never stop
People have survived atomic bombs dropped
Bypass the drug store for Botanica Shops
Grass is legal! There is still time to cop
Let the clouds entertain the mountain top
You were born training not to lose this bout
Tell us Eddie—What was the dream about?

Never forget death is all in the mind
Hurry up start admitting everything is fine
True we drank a lot But never really got blind
Revolutionized theatre for man & womankind
Puerto Rico isn't free yet You cannot resign
Jíbaro Sí! You must continue to always shout
Tell us Eddie—What was the dream about?

Your final performance is nowhere in sight
There can be no victory if there isn't a fight

Dreams do not always occur late at night
If you are never wrong you can never be right
Never again let the doctors get you uptight
Prove to them that you Were never down and out
Tell us Eddie—What was the dream about?

Only you can direct you into good health
By believing in you more than in yourself
Below the surface you will never find wealth
We will march again in Ponce with everyone else
Armed with history from El Barrio's book shelf
Where we learn to become our own spiritual scout
Tell us Eddie—What was the dream about!

Are you over the mountain Across the sea?
Hell No! You are still director of your destiny
As of lately you don't seem to feel so free
But that is the fault of that other society
The one that doesn't believe what it cannot see
You have the scheme & clues to keep death out
Tell us Eddie—What was the dream about!

Get off the downtown train it is going nowhere
The next stop will always be another nightmare
Only your mind can offer your body fresh air
Don't look at yourself expecting to be scared
The earth in your eyes will always be there
The New Rican Village is your eternal house
Tell us Eddie—What was the dream about?

The band continues playing your favorite song
Indicating that there is nothing wrong
If the past was weak the future looks strong
Dying can be fatal Dying where we don't belong

What is right today Tomorrow will be wrong
Our cultural Renaissance has survived the drought
Tell us Eddie—What was the dream about?

You always believed you had nothing to fear
Even when the end of time seemed to be near
You knew how to make Your problems disappear
By living in centuries far beyond your years
The meaning of immortality to you is quite clear
It will always be the 1st round of another bout
Tell us Eddie—What was the dream about?

There's no time to waste No time to lose
We have come too far to start singing the blues
Rebel against the medical dosage of bad news
Keep your eyes wide open for traditional clues
Of medicinal remedies our ancestors once used
Have confidence in the faith of the truly devout
Tell us Eddie—What was the dream about?

Deep rivers have to be crossed many times
50 years from now we'll still be in our prime
In your hometown dying is considered a crime
Great grandchildren will keep the vision sublime
They are the mountains we were born to climb
You must have an answer for them when they shout
Tell us Eddie—What was the dream about?

You will never be forsaken by the sun
Farewell is for those who have chosen to run
In times of sorrow we still managed to have fun
Disagreements were necessary to get the work done
Paradise is the state of mind we are all from

Earth is a kingdom that will never throw us out
Tell us Eddie—What was the dream about?

The reason why at this moment we now meet
Is to celebrate the downfall of defeat
And welcome the victory we were born to greet
Because our heart never skipped a beat
And taught us how to be strong and compete
In this great universe without fear or doubts
Right On Eddie—That's what the dream is about!

EL SPANGLISH NATIONAL ANTHEM

En my Viejo San Juan
They raise the price of pan
So I fly to Manhattan.
It was there that I swear
Everyone took welfare
Especially the Latins!

To El Barrio I went
In pursuit of low rent
In a five room apartment
Where my neighbors will be
Puerto Ricans like me
Dressed in tropical
garments.

I know
I know I know
Next stop's Puerto Rico
(So help me OTB
And so
And so And so
I won't be called Chico
By the Statue of Liberty)

Y thennnnn
Con familia y friends
Good times will never end
Learn how to laugh again
And stop sheeteen on ten
(Once in my country

Be-cosssss
I'm still in Puerto Rico
Only my body came
My strong spirit remains
Everything's still de same
(I truly do believe
You can leave and still be
Where Mami met Papi)

Some did assimilate
In de United States
They got rid of de accent
Though whenever they
spoke you knew who were
their folks

I know,
I know, I know
I'll miss Puerto Rico
(Land of de Palm trees)
And so,
And so and so
I'll live in El Barrio's
(Latin Community)

And whennnnn
I hit the numbers
I'll return to San Juan
Afford the price of pan
Until my vida is done

Many years came and went
Fell behind on the rent

I will be I will be
Who has always been me)

In Spanish there were bills
In English there were bills
That just kept getting
bigger.
Categorized as hicks
We were called dirty spicks
Blanco trash and black
niggers

Las botanicas saved
Us from an early grave
All aspirin did wass kill joo!
Muchas gracias Changó
La Plena y el Mambo

That will always unmask
them!

But de majority
Kept their identity
Never did lose their
accent!
They were proud not
ashamed
Of their Boricua names
If you don't believe ask
them.

I know
I know I know
I am being followed
(By my destiny)

Cursed Christopher
Columbus.
Worked as hard as I could
But my luck was no good
Never once hit the numbers

Now everyday I pray
Before passing away
And going six foot under

That again I will see
People who look like me
In my island of wonders.

I know
I know I know
I'll reach Puerto Rico
(Y live to be ninety three)
And so And so
Once in Puerto Rico
(Won't be a minority)

For coming to the rescue!

I know
I know I know
We have been in limbo
(Here in New York City)
And so
And so And so
Almost misplaced my soul
(Somewhere in New Jersey)

Porqueeeee blood is
Thicker than Coca-Cola
I have very high hopes
Of rejoining my folks
With them I'm never broke

We registered to vote

And so
And so And so
I will never be swallowed
(By inferiority)

And whennnnn
De plane takes off again
I know that there will be

No return trips for me
Back to New York City
(Island blessed by the sun
Here I come Here I come
Donde my roots are from)

And with my family
We'll struggle and believe
That one day we'll be free.

If I can't fly I'll swim
Straight from El Barrio
Back to Puerto Rico

De weather wasn't nice
Comfort cost a high price
Unlike in Puerto Rico
We kept cooking the rice
And re-heating the beans
And making cuchifrito.

De hard times were plenty
De pockets stayed empty
But the soul nunca
dyyyyyed
And junto we survived
And danced after we cried
Defending nuestro pride.

Thinking that there was
hope in elected officials.
Pero as soon as they win
For a moment they grin
Then they drop all the
issues.

Many dropped out of school
Others went to college
Trying hard to get
somewhere.
In the land of da free
Where without a degree
You cannot collect welfare.

I know
I know I know

Eeeeee!

De hard times were plenty
De pockets stayed empty
But the soul nunca
dyyyyyed
And junto we survived
And danced after we cried
Defending nuestro pride.

I'll always play dominoes
(Wherever I may be)
And go
And go And go
To local bodegas
(For Bustelo coffee)

EL PUERTO RICAN EMBASSY/MANIFESTO

We are a sovereign state of mind, well aware of the
fact that it is almost 1898 again and our own Embassy is
long overdue for the most interesting minds of our great
multicolorful generation to congregate as heads of state
and keep our aesthetic sancocho warm enough to escort
our eternal tropical contemporary urban lifestyle into the
21st Century phase of the pursuit of liberty & justice on
the dance floor of the happiness promised our existence
by the multi-lingo Spanglish creator of man and woman
kind!

Because war has never been on our agenda of survival.
Our only mission is to live and let live in peace &
harmony with all the citizens of the remarkable Planet
Earth. We hold no animosity against anyone, even after
400 years of endeavoring to be fluent in Spanish against
our will To then be instructed to learn English on short
notice for the next one hundred years by other total
strangers who are so impressed with our island that they
decided to stay and told us to leave and find a better way
of life.

El Puerto Rican Embassy is necessary if Puerto Ricans
are to be excluded from the list of endangered species.
Without it our destiny is at the mercy of foreign minds
who don't understand that the imagination has always
been an independent country with a spontaneous sense
of survival. It is there that the beginning of time became
relevant!

And why shouldn't we be Independent? We know how to sing and dance And paint And write poetry And educate each other. In the history of our memory of thousands of years ago We all remember being Taino Indians before Columbus Invaded our eternal beaches of everlasting, magnificent Resources the Earth provided the indigenous population of our Island. The power of memory eliminates the threat of extinction. We have no intention of forgetting who we were and who we are And will continue to be for now & forever & beyond!

Your body can't be free if your mind is still in prison. There is nothing original about you, you are practicing what someone else preaches which deprives your imagination of equal rights! And that is the biggest error committed against yourself and those who depend on you for knowledge.

Because the subconscious doesn't believe in collectivity individual dreams is what keeps the world from becoming aesthetically insignificant. Every individual has a secret down to earth harmless ulterior motive for staying alive and as long as it doesn't prevent others from allowing their dreams to come true there is nothing wrong with you and El Puerto Rican Embassy welcomes you with open arms regardless of your temporary political sentiments. *Vaya!*

Our surrealistic history has proven that we are immune to mediocrity! Therefore, the future has resourceful plans for us. Working together isn't impossible but inevitable! We are a Nation of one and many millions of eternal Ricans who need to visit each other more often to keep up with the latest bochinches in the artistic and political circles.

To be free means to be proud of yourself!
To be proud of yourself means to be creative!
To be creative means to defend your dreams!
To defend your dreams means to have the courage
To make your dreams come true in your lifetime!
And once your dreams come true you will never
Have to worry about dying as long as you live!

What do we want? What every human being wants! The right to dance la Plena whenever we please like dignified human beings of tropical brilliance who time after time their fine minds have proven that you can be in two islands at the same time Dancing to supernatural down to earth rhythms from Solitary jukeboxes from the past, present & future!

If we are to live forever it is imperative that we have an Embassy where we can all get together to share secrets of eternal life and acknowledge that we will always be related to each other in every artisitic discipline imagined!

We are not a government in exile! This is where we live! As a collective of indigenous survivors who have always voted for self-preservation wherever we have been located at the time of endeavoring to keep making ends meet. *Vaya!*

Ambassador Eduardo Figueroa said, "We are a Spirit Republic! No one understands a rainbow better than

Puerto Ricans who are a physical and spiritual
combination of all nations of the world. Everywhere you
travel you will meet yourself."

Everyone's imagination is a Sovereign Nation!
Freedom of expression has no boundaries to impede
The individual from reaching the other side while alive
To communicate with the dead & escort them back to life
To reassure us that we need no man's permission to be
free
To reassure us that we are dignitaries, *porque somos
Hermanos y hermanas* on the same side of the mirror
That our *Isla del Encanto* admirably stares at us from!

El Puerto Rican Embassy is necessary to explain How
our Rain Forest functions! And why we came here In the
first place. Not to better our standard of living But to
expand our vision of how the world really began And
celebrate the fact that we are all related to each other!

That's why our Proclamation of Independence Is nothing
to fear BUT something to enjoy together With whoever is
serious about living forever peacefully In the house of
everyone's universal ancestors: Earth! Which gives
everyone this day their daily identity. *Vaya!*

El Puerto Rican Embassy Manifesto
Rev. Pedro Pietri, 1994
Co-Director, El Puerto Rican Embassy

ODE TO A GRASSHOPPER
(I hope)

The only reason

That I am this pre-autumn

Afternoon in the privacy

Of my suspicious living room

Grant myself permission

To believe in god once again

Is solely because I saw

An unexpected grasshopper

Staring at my thoughts

On the table that keeps

The telephone from having

A mind of its very own

At first I was startled

And then I was startled less

At the sight of this insect

Put together in green details

To pay me an afternoon visit

39 floors above floor level

In my High Rise Hobo apartment

Miracle on 53rd street

Grasshopper hopped all the way

39 floors above floor level

To deliberately invade my privacy

And I didn't mind at all

After grasshopper assured me

It didn't speak English or Spanish

Or Chinese with an Italian accent

So we hit it off right away

You mind your own business

And I will not ask you

Any personal questions aside

From how the hell did you get here

I've never written a poem

About grasshoppers this high up before

And I know it wasn't something

My non existing paint brushes

Conceived behind my back and

The only grass I have here is

To smoke & not hop around in

Until I get dizzy and levitate

There has to be a mistake

Or did the grasshopper take

The elevator to the 39th floor

And enter my apartment without knocking

To make it obvious grasshoppers

Have the right to remain silent also

And give credit to the desert

For his arrival and not no Almighty

The only other mystery capable

Putting a grasshopper together from

Scratch if the clouds itch

I wish it had gone somewhere else

And keep religion out of my house

But no the grasshopper stopped here

And now I have to write about.

NIGHTTIME SUNSHINE MIND GAME

did she tell you
as she reads the cards
that your heart is
a foreign country
without borders to impede
love at first sight
on the last day of the universe?

did she tell you
that a secret overt admirer
who prefers to remain anonymous
all the nights of his illusions
detects eternity in eyes
that wear your delicate body?

did she tell you
he is constantly thinking
about constantly telling you
he constantly thinks about you
when he's pretending to sleep
after doubting another vision
of how he ended up lost
in the desert of his thoughts?

did she tell you
about an endless daydreamer
who spends all his spare time
fantasizing about your after-life
indicating that you will never
be absent from his inner conflict

long after you cease being fine
to then become fantastic!

did she tell you
he is capable of necrophilia
should you sleep late
the following morning
after finally meeting yourself
over the somewhere else rainbow
within walking distance from
a satisfaction that never comes

did she mention
a familiar undiscovered garden
where the flowers at all hours
are incredible and impossible
& the sublime season shines
in an everlasting summertime
inside of mirrors the night stares into

where the living stays easy
& ghost stories are fascinating
& the wine is victoriously red
& the history of eternal miseries
continues to repeat itself slowly?

did she tell you this?
did your finger tips tremble
as you suddenly remember meeting
in the perfumed valley of shadows
where the moon stays full forever
in a slow dream of fast dancing
& eternal romancing before dawn?

did she tell you to beware?
did she tell you to despair?
did she tell you to prepare
for clues leading to evidence
of immortality shortly after
the romance with death ends?

and last but not least
did she tell you that you have
the right to remain silent
or become a stranger yourself
aboard a spaceless ship that must sink
into your heart with him there
during an amazing discovery
of passion 2 personal 4 details

did she tell you this?
did she tell you all of this?
and if she didn't tell you this
then he is telling you this
& this is what he is telling you!

FREE GRASS FOR THE WORKING CLASS

Freelance serious circus workers
Of the inner circles of headlines
In reference to the latest crimes
Against the sanity of humanity
For which it staggers as opposed
To levitating for hesitating To
Feel nice enough about yourself
To solve your problems right now!

Quit your jobs before your jobs
Quit you and you are left with
Absolutely nothingwhatsoever to do
with the spare time of your mind

& regardless of how many times
You bring down the window shades
Your bill collectors won't go away
They will always be around to keep
Reminding you from nine to five
All you have to do is jump once

Into the prison of revolving doors
For inmates of economic paranoia
Who were sentenced to live forever
For sole purpose of making ends meet
Or get your ass thrown in the street

(all is quiet on the riot scene)

It is quiet because what goes up
Has at last came down from the trip

Of believing change is possible
Out side the impossible dream of
Ruling the world with good smoke
Signals from a spiritual Island
Off the coast of the heart & soul
Of seed that needs no introduction

Free grass for the working Class
(don't let the system kick your ass)
Free grass for the working class
(don't let the system kick your ass)

You conduct your own high mass
You are doing nothing wrong man
And woman of this promised land
To all who could and all who can

On the side of peace on earth stand!

And live to be a thousand years
Ahead of your interplanetary time
In the house of your inner feelings
Dealing with comfort & relaxation
In one nation under excellent smoke!

Being bored to death isn't a joke
Confined against your will to sing
Along with tv commercial jingles
Until the remote control drops dead
And you drag your remains to bed
Exhausted as all hell (unable to
Believe you are being deceived &
send the product straight to hell)

To bring the mind closer to Poets
Preventing the planet from extinction
By not paying their bills on time

To the goddamnfounding fathers
Of eternal air pollution for all!
Because America don't take no shit
From recent immigrants without money
& no choice but to mind their own
Business if they don't own a business
Paying the employees minimum wages
Until the imagination becomes vivid
And all hell breaks loose against

The state of mind of the mindless
No longer rushing to buy tokens.
Not that the mandatory oath of punk
Chewality was amended over night.
Metro cards are god's latest scheme
To fool the masses into believing
At last they are getting a free ride

And you better be quick about it
Cause there's a time limit to thee
Latest gimmick to keep you content
With existing just to pay your rent
& biblical bookie on time or else
You will also be talking nonsense

To yourself on any given insane
Asylum Island separating uptown
And downtown insane traffic lanes
Sitting on a park bench all alone

Never ever having to go home again
Now that you have nowhere to live

& You can't get your money back
All the banks are out to lunch
And won't be back anytime soon
From vacation on the half moon
But you still have to report to
Work On time or be deducted of
Your sanity for liberty & bigotry
In the land of the so called
Free to do whatever you please!

Where you aren't free at all
If you have to make ends meet
At a job you officially dispise
And your employer is the C.I.A.
Because if you aren't busy over

Overthrowing the goddamn system
You are busy keeping it in power!

Free grass for the working class
(don't let the system kick your ass)
Free grass for the working class
(don't let the system kick your ass)

Defend your imagination at home
Let no politician hear your poems
Tell your employer to go & screw
There is nothing wrong with you
The head you save will be your own

My fellow groovy proletarians
Meat eaters are also vegetarians
And heads of state are not heads
But boring motherfuckers instead
Who have committed the crime
Of outlawing having a nice time!

You not only deserve a break
Today (but every day of the week)
You should be allow to speak
A different foreign language man
(& woman & children & martians)

Should have the rite to lite up
Whatever they prefer to inhale
& not be sent to jail for smoking
And joking about the president
Who said he didn't when he did!

Yes I have flip my latino lid
Even though I speak no Latin
Everyone in Manhattan is insane
& the leaders are mentally ill
Which is worse than being crazy

At least lunatics have charisma
& only promise to laugh alot
When arrested for smoking pot
& the only confession (they'll
make) upon being finger printed
Is that what goes up stays up!

They don't believe they can fly
They are convinced they could

& you should also be convinced
The law of gravity can be broken
Even if you earn minimum wages.

Then everything will be fine
Then everything will be great
Then you will feel not guilty
About getting to work late
& not have a legitimate excuse
But a legitimate high alibi:

You forgot that you were poor

Taking a short thru the park
To get to work on time until
You cross the path of friends
Who had good grass to share.

Suddenly your problems were few
And the dream was about peace
There were no thoughts about war
And the poem wrote itself
And the painting painted itself
And the music played by itself
And you dance because you came
To dance & not to lose your mind
In all american assembly lines

Free grass for the working class
(don't let the system kick your ass)
Free grass for the working class
(don't let the system kick your ass)

The mission is to feel nice
And start a romance with life
Unite the past with the future
Stop discriminating against
The dead (ahead of their time)
& don't scream when they rise
& dance if they want to dance
& sing if they want to sing
With the living day and night

They who never left are back
To continue the main event
From the rent free red planet
Where there is no panic to
Make ends meet or cross from
One side of the continent
To the end of time and space
(not the end of the human race)
Exempt from the fire nextime

Convinced the grass is green
Convinced the grass is fine
Convinced the grass is serene
Convinced the grass is legal
Convinced the grass is free
Convinced the grass is magic
Convinced the grass is more
Powerful than pen and sword!

The revolution will come again
This time it will be more blunt
Rolled in a 50 cent philly cigar
In a world almost ruled by hip hop
To copy or not to cop & stop lies!

Adults must be accompanied by
Minors with underground rhymes
Or they will not be allowed into
The kingdom of improvisation
To celebrate the imagination

Single handedly responsible for
The collapse of all governments

Who opposed walking on the grass
Who opposed talking on the grass
Who opposed turning on the grass
In the land of the not so freeee

The only thing in this city
That is free is shock therapy
For the underclass under thee
Boardwalk mind of Coney Island
Side shows by seashore madness
War zone (monitored by secret
Agents) riding on the cyclone
With hidden microphone in ears
So tall they touch the clouds
& get electrocuted on the job
For God & private country club

Of autocratic cloud mechanics
Who almost got away with murder
Had they not been the ones who
Got killed by unfriendly fire
But didn't make the headlines

The reporters they reported
They saw nothing & went home

For fear of being handcuffed
By the bearded lady and then
Interrogated by the resident
Sword swallower & fire eater
Who will sentence you to be
Hung at Madison Square Garden!

Yo just turn to the sports
pages (& mind your own business)
If you want a raise & promotion
In a system that deceives you
Into believing you're receiving
Equal opportunity every now & then
To keep you quiet in the riots!

And that is why the church on
111th street & Lexington Avenue
Is still the church on 111th st.

(House of prayer & not progress)

Where angry Puerto Rican were
Allowed to be free from 1970
To 1973 & then had to disappear
To make ends meet the next year

& El Barrio went back to its
Daily educational Dominoe games
To keep traditions Alive & well
And the hell with politicians
From the left & right & middle
Who know cigarette smoking is

Hazardous to your health (but)
Still refuse to outlaw tobacco

To take the future out of
Our future & prepare us all
To declare war on each other
Until all avenues are foreign
And everyone will get lost
Once they leave the apartment
Of their forgotten home address
And end up a total stranger
On the street where they live

And that happens to everyone
Who doesn't believe that thee
Bow & Arrow is mightier then
Their godless word processor
Where novels occur overnight
Even if they are not written

And they were not written if
They were not written on "A"
Manual typewriter purchased
From the historical stoops of
Harmonizing Acapela radical
Rock and Roll Singing groups!

Free grass for the working class
(don't let the system kick your ass)
Free grass for the working class
(don't let the system kick your ass)

Few are chosen to understand
Anything! says the panhandler

With his underground saxophone
Greater metropolitan jazz accent
Of disillusioned hip musician
Who will be coming from Mars
As soon as he hits the lotto.

The Soviet Union never fell
The KGB is still around
The United States collapsed
The homeless are the proof
On the Times Square Shuttle
The latest house of Detention
The later it never becomes

The Panhandler swears is true
Even if it isn't true just yet!
Only one person allowed to be
Making chump change on train
Of thoughts not to be divulged

No one knows who they are
No one knows where they are
No one knows what they are
No one knows when they are
No one knows that they are
No one knows why they are
No one knows how many they are?

The only sane person in nyc
Is Alex the GreeCan from
Latin Manhattan and Greece
Street vendor of hot dogs
& sausages & pretzels and
ShishKabob on lonely stick

& Knishes & cans of soda too
to keep you cool in hell
not far from hell's kitchen!

Never ask the Greek Rican
How Does he makes ends meet?
Be content by just knowing
He is one of us who supports
& will never stop supporting:

Free Grass for the Working class
Free Grass for the working class
Free grass for the working class

Later for laws that are passed
To keep the working class
Off the grass & all that jazz!

Listen up & Listen good bro
Is cool to make ends meet
Without selling your soul
To the Surgeon Virgin General
& that is all you have to know!
The street Poet told you so

Before disconnecting his phone
To let it be offcially knowned
This is the twilight zone
& Rudy Guiliani isn't the mayor

Baseball players run New York
And every other major cities
Where the homeless aren't pity

And the laws of the city suck
And the politicians suck
And the police officers suck
And the parking meters suck
And the transit system sucks
And you can never make a buck!

Free grass for the working class
(don't let the system kick your ass)
Free grass for the working class
(don't let the system kick your ass)

If you decide to decide
To reach the other side alive
by growing your own grass
You are not committing a crime
You are just refusing
Refusing to commit suicide

Because grass is not illegal
What is illegal is arresting
Everybody for appreciating grass!

On your coffee break
On your lunch break
On your snack break
On your toilet break
On your broken back break
On your aching neck break
On your two weeks vacation
On your retirement celebration

Make your favorite color green)

And what all this means
Is that we as human beings
Are endowed with the inalienable
Right to light up when we feel
The holiday season is unreal
& we have to do something about
How manic the weather can get
The darker the days become
And the clearer the night sees

As we walk or we levitate
To reach the undivided ocean
On the other side of the mirror
When we shut our eyes to see
How incredible being high can be

As we leave our foot prints
On the mysterious blue sands
Of foreign subconscious beach
Until we get lost & are found
Safe and sound on the path
Of the mountain that can only
Be climbed very late at nite
Following the clues of dream
Coming true before dreams begins

To divulge the secret keeping us
Calm in the valley of the privacy
Of our imagination in one nation
Under good smoke for all at last!

Free grass for the working class
Don't let the system kick your ass)

Free grass for the working class
Don't let the system kick your ass)

Your problems will come to pass
Celebrate your own high mass
Free grass for the working class!

LOST IN THE MUSEUM OF NATURAL HISTORY

It was nice day at the beach. The hottest day of the summer, the temperature was in the 90's. A record-breaking crowd from all corners of the metropolitan disaster areas where it stays very cold all year around came out on this extremely hot Saturday to socialize with the sun, whose fever was incredible. Honest hard workers from neighborhoods that are hazardous to your health escaping the agony and eternal aggravation of the asphalt battlegrounds their below average standards of living have confined them to. Today their bill collectors will be buried in unmarked graves in mental cemeteries. The only recollection they will have of their endless miserable living conditions will be the combinated numbers they played early in the morning before coming to the beach in uncomfortable public transportation or used cars whose batteries went dead in highway traffic jams.

This is an integrated beach, there are poor people and poorer people with identical economic problems seeking oblivion from the predicament of making financial ends meet in a capitalistic society manipulated by a handful of aristocratic criminals disguised as benevolent politicians to keep the problems oppression creates from encountering a solution.

For some it will be the first and last time that they will come to the beach this summer. The trip is too expensive to take more than once if your local fortune teller is having a consistent streak of unreliable predictions. These are the ones in the category of "poorer people" who will chew their bread and butter picnic lunches from the time they get to the beach until it is time to return to the vicinity where destruction is inevitable. The poor people can come back a few more times because they are assistant supervisors and have a better credit rating with the urban loan sharks who will never be caught dead or alive in public beaches where it's impossible to swim a few inches without cracking your skull from headon collisions because the ocean is over-populated.

But, aside from the discomforts and disadvantages of low income recreation, you can still have a fairly decent time at the beach if you have a vivid imagination that will take you to places you can never afford to visit if you were travelling under conventional circumstances.

Back in the early 1950s, when I was still under the jurisdiction of old time religion and impossible dreams after being indoctrinated by triple feature western flicks and repetitive cartoons shown at the West End Theatre on 125th Street in between Morningside and St. Nicholas Avenues in uptown Manhattan, there was enough space available on the beach for those who will never make the major leagues or become the heavyweight champion of the world to fantasize about being famous. But now, 20 years and many endless hangovers later it is different, there is standing room only if you get there early or late.

Old teenagers and young senior citizens were having a nice time. Everywhere you looked, everybody was busy eating and talking about what they were going to eat next. People ate on the boardwalk, in the sand, asleep and awake, taking a sun tan; they ate swimming above and under water; they ate regardless of what recreational activities they indulged in.

The most eating was done at the outdoor cafeteria where I sit alone on the seat of a table with an opened beach umbrella on top, writing down notes for future references and eating an imaginary heroe sandwich.

The fragile voice of a 5-year-old little girl is heard calling for her mother. "Mommy, Mommy, where are you?" She has jet black curly hair and is wearing a white first communion ankle-length dress. Everybody at the beach hears the helpless child, but they are too busy eating to pay her any attention. She has been lost for a few hours and is very hungry and thirsty, walking in a daze looking for her mother who she was separated from in the process of closing and opening her eyes.

A mixed couple (man and woman) sharing a hot dog approach the little girl and ask her, "Are you really lost?"

"Yes, I cannot find my Mommy," the little girl tells them. The mixed couple burst out laughing and walk away from her to look for something else to eat. I am almost tempted to offer the little girl my assistance in locating her missing mother, but since I am making this story up there is nothing I can do to help her, even though she is about to pass out from heat exhaustion.

Staggering from table to table at the cafeteria, she begs for food and water and information on the where-abouts of her mother. "Get the hell out of here!" is the only response she gets. When she comes toward my table she sees nobody there, and walks onto the boardwalk, desperate for help.

Everybody on the beach is wearing shoes except the little girl, who is lost or could have been abandoned for bugging her parents about the high cost of living these crucial times of interplanetary income taxes for the kingdom and the glory of a.c. and d.c. current. Swimmers wear shoes also. The victim of circumstances beyond her control is violently pushed and shoved and laughed at by everybody she implores help from on the boardwalk. A group of musicians from the Salvation Army chases her into the sand playing hymns of salvation on their religious instruments.

Running at full speed to avoid being converted, the little girl joins a motorcycle gang getting high below the surface close to the ocean, armed and dangerous with framed portraits of their motorcycles instead of the real thing. She gets stoned with them drinking wine and smoking dynamite grass. I have a pint of Puerto Rican rum from Ponce that I am drinking from at intervals in between punctuations on my notes for future reference. Wine is unkind to the mind. I have no emotional use for it. It instigates headaches and induces depression. Rum is articulate.

Accidently tripping after over somebody's absurd grandmother, who is flat on her back sunbathing in a two-piece bathing suit, wearing shades and a transistor radio helmet on her head, tuned into rock and rolles music, also chewing on her breakfast, lunch or last supper. The child jumps for joy on noticing the person she tripped over is her missing in action mother. "Mommy, Mommy, I found you, thank goodness!" She goes over to embrace her mother.

"Get away from me!" her mother shouts as she pushes her daughter to the ground.

"Hey, bitch, what seems to be your problem? Aren't you glad to see me safe and sound?" she asks her mother, who is enjoying the fact that she had lost her daughter at the beach.

"Hell no, I am not glad to see you. I told you when we left for the beach this morning that if you got lost you'd better stay lost, so get lost, I never want to see you again as long as I live!"

"That is no way for a grown woman to be behaving, you are obligated to me, you are my provider, my development depends on your principles, your guidance is a necessity throughout this mysterious experience honey, for accepting the assignment of being my biological mother."

"You smell like you've been drinking alcoholic beverages," her mother shouts as she smacks her across the face with all her might.

A parade of midgets in military uniforms rides skateboards in the sweltering sand. Each has a portable radio tuned into a different station at full blast. As I type these notes for future reference a few weeks from now in my furnished room on the Upper West Side, I notice a beautiful woman in the window across from mine, half naked and exceptionally fine, with an eternal sad expression on her face because when she was very young everybody who was born this year was very old and hung out at the Bureau of Missing Immaculate Persons.

"But Mommy, I only drank because I was lonely," the little girl cries. A bisexual senior citizen on a remote controlled wheelchair snatches my notes and takes off in his wheelchair at 30 miles per hour, knocking down whoever gets in front of him. I get my notes back by throwing away the page I wrote that paragraph on. The little girl faints from getting hit so hard. Her mother lights up a filter-tip cigarette and tries to make her daughter regain consciousness by burning cigarette holes in her arm.

"Aren't you hot with that hat on?" a hunchback beauty queen asks me as she crosses my path. "Aren't you hot with that bathing suit on?" I reply. Promise the fans sleeping pills if you want the attendance to pick up for the next game. This started out to be a picnic away from the picnic I was umbrella man in residence at. Had you become a radio and television mechanic like you started out to be, you too would be getting wet right now instead of distorting mundane incidents.

Everybody on the beach is laughing as the mother desperately tries to snap her daughter out of suspended animation with the lit cigarette, so she can smack her some more for drinking on the job of existing. She snaps out of it laughing louder than everybody else. "Mommy, I am very hungry and very thirsty, please give me something to eat and drink before I faint again," the little girl pleads with her mother.

"Are you still a virgin?" her mother demands to know.

"Yes ma'am, the gang only carried portraits of motorcycles, not the real thing."

"Okay you little bastard, I've had all I can take from you," her mother shouts. She goes into her handbag, brings out a switchblade knife and chases her daughter away from the spot where she was sunbathing. The crowd gives her a standing ovation for defending herself against the younger generation, who are convinced they have all the answers to questions nobody asked them.

From my table at the outdoor cafeteria, where I am sitting, writing down notes for future reference, I can see everything that is happening clearly: A baseball game has been postponed because one of the ball players is mentally ill and sees Martians in the outfield with Polaroid cameras snapping pictures of a traffic jam on an upside down bridge the night after New York City was left without electricity, complete a one-act play God was writing to become rich and famous because he had failed the Post Office examination, and outside civil service, the theater offers the next best benefits for those who are willing to sacrifice their sanity to become catatonically successful in the science of entertainment.

The little girl is lost again. She walks toward the salty ocean and drinks the salt water after swallowing a handful of wet sand. A priest in full uniform approaches the little girl. He goes into his holy pocket and bring out a handful of candy and offers it to the little girl, who has wet sand all over her mouth and cheeks. When she extends her hand to take the candy, the priest hides it behind his back and bends over to whisper something into the child's ear. She shakes her head in approval at what the priest is suggesting. She shuts her eyes and prepares her lips to be kissed by the priest in exchange for the candy he is withholding from her. When their lips are about to make contact, the priest backs away from her, disgusted. "Your breath stinks!" he says to her. She starts laughing loudly. The priest gets uptight and puts handcuffs on her and blindfolds her with his white collar. The crowd mobs the priest to get his autograph.

A religious fanatic with big tits and firm buttocks in an orange choir robe threatens to pee on my notes for future reference if I do not omit the role of the priest from this short story. I omit her instead, and follow the uptight priest with his 5-year-old prisoner into a pay toilet where her mother is found moving her bowels and screaming because she has lost her daughter on the beach. Police officers try to calm her down with their nightsticks. When the mother sees her daughter she throws herself at her and showers her with kisses, and holds her so very tight that she gets nauseous and vomits and gets slapped in the face. The priest writes the mother out a bill for finding her lost child, the police officers instigate her into beating the hell out of the little girl for causing her so much trouble, which she gladly does.

The little girl wishes she had stayed lost as her mother beats her mercilessly. I put my hands over my ears to avoid hearing her scream while everybody else at the beach is laughing. In the distance the siren of an ambulance is heard. This draws to the conclusion that tragedies are never spontaneous, they are always anticipated.

The bases are loaded, the next batter at the plate is batting 597, the count is 3 balls and no strikes, there are no outs, the next pitch is about to be delivered, tomorrow's headlines printed a few weeks ago have the batter hitting into a triple play.

Everybody chews their food faster while the little girl gets beat up by the person who loves her the most. She pleads with her mother to at least remove the handcuffs, so she can defend herself. But her mother is having too much fun to hear anything. She is really enjoying it.

Again I am tempted to go to the little girl's rescue. This time I rise from my seat and start heading in the direction of the massacre determined to defend the helpless child at the risk of being accused of talking to myself. But halfway there I change my mind and return to my table.

The little girl begs me to stop being so negative with my

imagination and write about the bright side of life. I pay her no attention because I am totally broke. This story has to be written regardless of whose feelings get hurt. This is the way I make my living. If I am unreliable to my fantasies the rent will not get paid.

The gentleman driving the ambulance started out his career in the circus as an attendant in a hospital for terminally ill mannequins, victims of a fatal disease called "Reality." There is no cure for this sickness, once you become real you stop existing. Those were some very unpleasant years for the ambulance driver —emptying out pissy bedpans, cleaning up shit every time the mannequins moved their bowels, because once you become real you also become helpless and shit on yourself.

The hours were long, the salary was inadequate, there were no chances of getting promoted to a ward of transvestites. So one melancholy day at the job, the frustrated attendant decided to commit suicide. He jumped out the window and landed on the driver's seat of an ambulance, dressed like a carnival derelict who had just fallen off a church altar.

Death comes to the rescue of the badly beaten little girl, now lost forever to all the pleasant and unpleasant experiences of existence. She was only with us on this good earth for a short time. She became a total stranger to her shadow before she fully understood the reflection she communicated with whenever she was interviewed by mirrors. Fate deprived her of self-expression, her politics will never be known, her unwritten love poems will never be published, her opinion on the subject of prostitution will be buried with her undeveloped figure, history will be unable to inform future generations if she was going to be flatchested or have breasts for movie producers to play with. She was the unfortunate victim of child abuse, her mother loved her so much that she beat her to death for getting lost at the beach.

I stop writing down notes for future reference to start

crying for a few seconds. Everybody at the beach is now wearing black armbands (and still eating). The ambulance is heard coming to a reckless halt on the boardwalk. The driver gets out and runs toward the cafeteria straight up to my table with an angry expression on his face.

"What the hell do you think you're doing, dressing me up like a clown when I'm supposed to be an ambulance driver, huh?" he says to me with his fists clenched in preparation to strike a fatalistic blow if his question doesn't receive a satisfactory answer.

"You are not the writer, you are being written about, you do not have the right to protest in what image you have been created, chump," I tell the ambulance driver, ready to hit him with my half full pint of rum in case he makes an attempt to strike me.

"I want to be dressed like an ambulance driver, not a commercial clown. My co-workers do not take me serious in this ridiculous outfit you have chosen for me to wear in this nonsense short story you are writing."

"Get back to work or else I will drop you from the story completely, and see to it that you never work again in my fantasies!" I shout to the ambulance driver, who then attacks me, and we roll onto the floor in hand-to-hand combat. A crowd gathers around us to watch me fight with myself. I am losing the fight so I stab him with a pencil eraser to avoid being humiliated by a figment of my imagination.

The manager of the cafeteria announces over a public address system that they are now selling frozen toy dolls of the little girl who got lost at the beach, with or without the handcuffs.

The ambulance driver is taken back to his ambulance mortally wounded on his own stretcher. His last words are, "Why don't you take off your clothes and go swimming like everybody else who came to the beach?"

I had all intention of doing that, but since nobody made a pass at me when I got here, I changed my mind about being mediocre and started writing down notes for future reference. I am not anti-social, I am anti-preliminaries. I want to swallow my food first and then chew it.

The child goes to Heaven and falls into a fit of depression the first half hour there. She misses the motorcycle gang badly. There is nothing to do in Heaven but ride the ferris wheel to the tune of "Auld Lang Syne."

She begs me through mental telepathy to bring her back to life, so that she can grow up to become a good sinner and go straight to Hell the next time she gets lost at the beach. I give in to her demands after making her promise me that she will let me take her to her high school prom. Presto! The little girl comes back to life with a few broken ribs, a fractured skull and a broken heart from the beating she received.

All the black armbands are removed and left on top of my table. The defunct ambulance driver has no complaints about his destiny, he is doing stand-up comedy in Purgatory and does not want to be resurrected from the dead to work again from 9 to 5 and be buried alive in the rush hours. I can't say I blame him. I worked for 10 years myself at odd jobs to make ends meet, and it was the biggest mistake I ever committed.

There is no future in working for anybody but yourself. You are the only one who will never hurt your feelings. Whatever profits you make you will share with yourself. Baseball players of the world unite!

The captain of the motorcycle gang, who is a mean-looking trans-sexual, comes over to my table and whispers something into my ear which I can't write about because that did not really happen.

And furthermore, this outdoor cafeteria is really a rented submarine from the Fulton Fish Market. If you put your hands through the air you will be temporarily blinded by un-identified underwater flying objects.

Riding the overcrowded airless hot-as-hell subway train on my way home from the beach after running out of notes to take down for future reference, I find myself still think-ing about the incident at the beach where everybody ate and talked about what they would eat after they were through eating. At this precise moment, the little girl who was lost and found is on the critical list at the intensive care unit in a hospital somewhere in the middle-class section of Brooklyn, recovering from the near-fatal beating her mother gave her for getting lost.

The motorcycle gang she joined to avoid being con-verted are the only ones at her bedside. There are poster-size photos of motorcycles on the walls of the room. The gang is getting high, as usual. When they reach the point of total incoherency they start removing the bandages and the intra-venous equipment from the little girl's badly beaten body. They put heavy make-up on her face and dress her up in the gang's eternal outfit.

An old lady on the subway train begs me to let her have my seat. I tell her, "Get lost, can't you see I am daydreaming!" Everybody on the train gives me a dirty look. I couldn't care less, I am almost through with this short story, they will very soon become unreal again and lose sleep looking for some-body else to make them a citizen of their fantasy.

The little girl leaves the hospital with the motorcycle gang. She is completely recovered and has forgiven me for putting her through all these unusual unpleasant unrealistic changes. I am a few stops away from my destination. I in-struct the little girl to knock hard on the door of her home very late at night, slightly intoxicated, still wearing the heavy make-up.

"Get your ass in this house, wash your face and go

straight to bed, you good for nothing brat! It's 3 in the morning, you have no business being out in the streets this late!" her mother says to her upon answering the door.

"Yes Mommy," the little girl says with her hand over her mouth so her mother will not smell the liquor on her breath. "Do you have a cigarette you can spare me, kid?" her mother asks her. She goes into the pocket of her motorcycle jacket, brings out a pack of Cigarettes and gives one to her mother, who takes the whole pack away from her.

The only lady who wants my seat on the train faints melodramatically. My conscience starts bothering me. I apologize to her as I omit her from my notes for future reference. Everybody on the train smiles at me.

The little girl is in bed, sound asleep. Her mother is watching the Late Late Show on a portable television set inside the refrigerator, so she will not miss a second of the program in case she wants something to munch on. Somebody is heard knocking on her door. She rises, shuts the refrigerator door, and goes to answer the door. A man and a woman wearing winter overcoats, gloves and fur hats greet her warmly.

"Hi Ma," the woman says to her as they walk into the apartment, still trembling from the cold weather outside. "How did everything go with our little girl?" the man asks.

"Everything went just fine. I took her to the Museum of Natural History and she enjoyed it very much."

"I'm sorry we're late Ma, the movie was longer than we expected," the woman apologizes.

"Don't worry about it, as long as you enjoyed yourself that's all that matters. I have nothing to complain about. I had a wonderful time with my granddaughter. She's such a sweet adorable child, gave me no trouble at all."

The train stops at the station where I'm supposed to get off. I purposely miss my stop to finish the story.

"Take off your coats, sit down and get yourself warmed up while I go to prepare some hot coffee for you." The little girl is heard screaming in the bedroom. All three adults rush to the bedroom to find out what's the matter. They go over to the little girl in bed and comfort her.

"What's wrong with Mommy's little baby?" the younger lady asks with a frightened expression on her face.

"I had a dream that a man dressed in black was writing a strange story about me."

When the train stops again I have all intentions of getting off, but when I try to move nothing happens, my body is motionless, I am unable to get up. The little girl I am writing about enters the train to distribute gypsy business cards. When she comes to where I am hopelessly seated she hands me one of the cards she is distributing, and quickly draws her hand back when I reach out for it, and proceeds to the next passenger coming home from the beach.

EDITOR'S NOTE

It is a great pleasure for each of us to edit the poetry of Pedro Pietri and make it available to the broad reading public, especially as we do so on the personal request of Pedro Pietri himself. In December 2003, a few months before his death, our dear friend Pedro summoned us to his sister Carmen's house in the Bronx and, in her presence, asked us if we would be willing to take charge of the edition of his poems. We were both honored and delighted at the prospect, and now, almost eleven years later, we have finally brought the project to completion with the present volume. We have chosen with great care and love what appeared to us the best work among his previously published books, *Puerto Rican Obituary* and *Traffic Violations*. These books are out of print and difficult to find. On the other hand, *Out of Order*, a massive book of approximately 3,000 poems, was an extremely limited, photocopied author's edition. We include here a representative sample that will help the reader ascertain Pietri's wit and humor. We also spent many hours in the Archives of the Centro de Estudios Puertorriqueños reading through the vast amount of unpublished material, some in the form of notes and jottings scattered in very informal places. The result of such effort is included under the headings *El Party Continues*, *Love Poems to My Surrealist Gypsy*, and *Loose Poems*. Except where clarity or meaning seemed compromised, no editing or corrections were made to Pietri's poems. We have arranged them in a very rough chronological order as far as we could determine. In arriving at our selection we have sought to give priority to the poetic work that seems to us to be the most enduring and treasured among his many writings In doing so, we decided to include his little known short story, "Lost in the

Museum of Natural History," as the final text of the selection. This particular text, published in 1981 in an extremely limited edition, although written in prose, underscores Pietri's poetic creativity and encompasses many of the major themes and ideological concerns found in previous works such as *Puerto Rican Obituary*. It highlights the continuities and connections found throughout his poetry. While we much admire his theatrical work, and of course his inimitable presence as a public performer, we have followed his suggestion and limited this publication to his poetry. For we feel that it is as a poet that Pedro Pietri will last forever in the minds and hearts of the Puerto Rican people, and of readers everywhere. May this modest effort on our part help establish the beloved Pedro Pietri as an immortal treasure of humanity.

We wish to acknowledge the people who helped make this book a reality.

To Margarita Deida, Pedro's widow and the administrator of his estate, for the permission granted to publish the selection. To his sister, Carmen Pietri, for supporting the project from the start. To Genette Lake, who carefully and respectfully typed the final draft. And to Ria Julien, who guided us through the legal hurdles and to the doors of City Lights Publishing. Our debt of gratitude to all for understanding the literary, cultural, and historical significance of Pedro Pietri's poetry.